I'M MOVIN' ON
THE LIFE AND LEGACY OF
HANK SNOW

VERNON OICKLE

NIMBUS
PUBLISHING LTD

Nimbus Publishing Limited
3731 Mackintosh St, Halifax, NS B3K 5A5
(902) 455-4286 nimbus.ca

Printed and bound in Canada

NB1080

Cover photo: Courtesy of the Friends of Hank Snow Society Collection, Liverpool, Nova Scotia
Interior and cover design: Jenn Embree

Library and Archives Canada Cataloguing in Publication

Oickle, Vernon, 1961-, author
I'm moving on : the life and legacy of Hank Snow / Vernon Oickle.
Issued in print and electronic formats.
ISBN 978-1-77108-138-2 (pbk.).—ISBN 978-1-77108-139-9 (pdf).
—ISBN 978-1-77108-140-5 (mobi).—ISBN 978-1-77108-141-2 (html)

1. Snow, Hank, 1914-1999. 2. Country musicians—United States—Biography. I. Title.

ML420.S674O39 2014   782.421642092   C2013-908096-1
                                                    C2013-908097-X

Nimbus Publishing acknowledges the financial support for its publishing activities from the Government of Canada through the Canada Book Fund (CBF) and the Canada Council for the Arts, and from the Province of Nova Scotia through Film & Creative Industries Nova Scotia. We are pleased to work in partnership with Film & Creative Industries Nova Scotia to develop and promote our creative industries for the benefit of all Nova Scotians.

for

Jimmie Rodgers Snow

and

Sheri Blackwood

CONTENTS

FOREWORD

My Father, Hank Snow

When *Vernon asked* me to do the foreword for his new book I was extremely delighted, but at the same time very nervous. My father had such a vast career and there were so many different directions that I could go. I didn't even know where to begin. Since Vernon did such a magnificent job in researching my father's life for this book, I'll see if I can fill in some gaps here and there. I'll start by going back to the beginning, when I was a child.

It wasn't easy in those early days due to the fact that my father had less than a sixth-grade education, and most people thought that trying to become a star and a recording artist was pretty much out of the question. But Dad was a very persistent individual, which was one of his great qualities. He was a very determined person and no matter what the cost, he would see it through.

Dad had a lot of disappointments in those early days, which resulted in him drinking. He became a heavy drinker, which made it very difficult on Mother and I, especially given the fact we never had one particular place we could call home. I think the one thing that stands out the most in my mind is of the weeks we had to live in my Dad's truck with a horse and two dogs. I remember there was a little bed that was over top of the driver's cabin where we used to sleep. I can shut my eyes and still see Dad reaching across this small area every night before we went to sleep. Dad would slide this little door to one side and give lumps of sugar to the horse, Shawnee. I'm really not sure why this picture stands out in my mind, but it does.

Our life changed in 1948 when Dad sent for us to join him south of the border. It was quite an ordeal when Mother and I entered the United States of America. It was in the month of March when we made our way by train all the way from Halifax to Port Huron, Michigan, and then on to Dallas, Texas. Dad was working in two nightclubs at that time and they were a kilometre apart. In the shows, he would put Shawnee through his routine and then sing songs to the drunks.

One interesting story I remember from that time in Texas is that one of those nightclubs was owned by the (later) infamous Jack Ruby. I remember meeting the man and would see him from time to time. What a shock it was for me when years later I would see this same man on national TV after assassinating Lee Harvey Oswald.

I also remember that on the weekends in Texas Dad performed on the Big D Jamboree, a smaller version of the world-famous Grand Ole Opry. It was at this time that things changed for him: when he met Ernest Tubb, who was a guest on Big D. Although my father and Ernest corresponded for many years, they had never actually met until this particular Saturday in 1948 and they instantly became lifelong friends. The common denominator for them was their love for the music of Jimmie Rodgers, known as the Father of County Music, after whom I was named.

Ernest was responsible for getting my father on the Grand Ole Opry for a tryout. If I recollect, it was only an eight- or ten-week try-out, and the Opry was going to let Dad go. Well on the heels of this dismissal, "I'm Movin' On" hit the airways and became a smash hit (as well as his signature song throughout his life). After that, things were different for us.

I am now seventy-seven, and as I look back over all these years of travelling with my dad, I appreciate that it was a great time in my life. Though it had its ups and downs and its sad times, if I had it to do all over again I don't think I would change a thing.

As I ponder my father's remarkable career, and view the legacy he left behind, this is what comes to mind. He spent forty-five years on one major label, RCA Victor. To date, no one has broken that record. I doubt it will ever be broken, especially today, with artists moving from one label to another. During this time he recorded 883 singles and 140 albums, and charted 85 singles on Billboard country charts. He had a career of six decades, during which he sold more then 80 million albums. He is a member of seven halls of fame in Canada and the U.S. No one else has yet been able to achieve this record.

Dad's greatest accomplishment was the forty-four weeks he spent on the music charts, in the top ten with one song. The music industry has changed so much, and today there are so many artists that a hit song doesn't last very long in the top ten. It is quite possible that dad's song "I'm Movin' On" will stand the test of time, and that his twenty-one weeks at number one will never be broken.

What a legacy for a man from Brooklyn, Nova Scotia; an abused child with a fifth-grade education, who went from being a cabin boy on a fishing boat to a country music superstar, and who set the pace for all who follow.

That's my father, Hank Snow!

Jimmie R. Snow

Jimmie Rodgers Snow

PREFACE

When *I was a* youngster growing up in Liverpool, Nova Scotia, there was an eight-by-ten, coloured photograph taped to the inside cover of our family photo album. As the scrapbook mostly contained photos of family members, I naturally concluded that the man depicted in this particular image was one of the family. However, when I asked, my dad promptly informed me that the man was Hank Snow.

Who Hank Snow was and what he meant to the world of country music was still a mystery to me at that time, but I could tell from the proud way my dad spoke that this was an important man, someone whose success we should celebrate as a community. It wasn't until I was much older and working as a journalist in my hometown that I fully understood the true stature of the man depicted in that photograph from my childhood.

Today we know Hank Snow as a legend in country music, a singer, songwriter, and world-class entertainer whose legions of fans still appreciate his style and honest storytelling. In his time, Snow was an international superstar, blazing a trail that few other Canadians—indeed, few others, period—had travelled before him. As his son, Jimmie, mentions in his foreword, Snow was inducted into seven halls of fame, held the longest recording contract of any artist in the history of recorded music, and to this day, decades after his death, holds the record for the song with the most consecutive weeks at number one on the Billboard Country Music charts—all testaments to his success.

This book is a tribute to the man who clawed his way from a troubled childhood of poverty and abuse to take his place on the

A promotional picture of Hank Snow from the 1960s.

world's stage, and establish himself as a legend in country music. Hank Show is proof that with drive, commitment, talent, and sheer determination, it is possible to achieve one's dreams.

This book would not have been possible without the gracious support and generosity of the following people who opened their lives and shared their stories about Hank Snow, starting with the folks at the Hank Snow Home Town Museum in Liverpool, and notably manager Kelly Inglis, who proved to be a valuable resource.

Kayton Roberts and Roger Carol, the last two remaining members of Hank Snow's Rainbow Ranch Boys (as of 2014), and Hank's close friend Marge Hemsworth also provided memories to help tell this story, as did longtime fan Larry Gaum, and Dirk van Loon and Frank Babin, two of the driving forces throughout the 1980s and '90s who helped establish the museum in Hank's hometown. Entertainers Mark Brine and (fellow Nova Scotian) Carroll Baker also answered the call for assistance when asked, and they have my deepest thanks and respect.

I also owe a great debt to both Hank's son, Jimmie Rodgers Snow, and to his long-time personal assistant and close friend, Sheri Blackwood. It is through them that I gained a better appreciation of Hank Snow—the person, the family man, the entertainer, the businessman, the country music legend—and it is for that reason that this book is equally dedicated to them.

Special thanks to my wife, Nancy Oickle, whose assistance with research, fact checking, and keeping me focused were valuable throughout this process. A final note of thanks to my publisher, Patrick Murphy; extraordinary book editors, Penelope Jackson and Whitney Moran; and to all the hard-working, talented people at Nimbus who helped make this book a reality.

MAY 9, 1914

The Early Years

Clarence Eugene Snow was born on May 9, 1914, in the small village of Brooklyn, Queens County. Located near Liverpool on Nova Scotia's rugged South Shore, the seaside hamlet boasted a population of roughly seven hundred residents at the time, many of whom were employed in the fishing and forestry industries. Struggling under the oppression that is poverty's partner, life was not easy for the Snow family, but it was particularly difficult for the young boy who seemed to never fit in anywhere.

Described as a scrawny and sickly youngster, Clarence was the fifth of six children born to George Lewis Snow and Marie Alice Boutlier. Within the first year of their births, the first two Snow children, Max and Olive, died of natural causes. Two sisters, Lillian and Nina, entered the world ahead of Clarence, and another sister, Marion, was born after him. Throughout his life Clarence maintained very close ties to his siblings, and no matter where he travelled, their bonds remained strong. Early on, the other children in the village took to calling him "Jack" for some unknown reason, and the nickname stuck after being adopted by family and friends, following him well into his teenaged years.

It was a rough start for the young boy who would someday go on to become an international country music legend, selling millions of records, singing and performing on stages around the globe before throngs of adoring fans and in front of heads of state. Jack had a long road to travel before he would reach that point.

Hank's Mother, Marie Alice Snow, c.1920s.

With none of today's modern conveniences and even less money at the average person's disposal, the early 1900s were difficult. The world had just been thrust into a global conflict following the outbreak of the First World War and the global economy was in tatters, leading to scarce job opportunities and rampant poverty throughout North America. Canada was not immune to the effects and small, rural communities like Brooklyn were hit especially hard as jobs dried up and virtually disappeared, leaving many in a destitute state.

As they were for most everyone else during this era, times were tough for the Snow family. Work was hard to come by, and although both parents laboured to maintain their household and feed their four children, it was a challenge. Still, they struggled through the obstacles that circumstances placed before them and somehow managed to at least provide the basics. There were no extras or luxuries, however, in the Snow household. Food staples and shelter were the top priorities; survival was the first order of business for everyone.

While scarce, happiness could be found in different ways. During Jack's early childhood, his father, George, imparted his fondness for the outdoors. In winter, he taught the children to skate and showed Jack how to hunt. George also passed his love of music onto his children, but especially to his only son. In his later life, Jack would come to appreciate this early exposure to music, and he'd credit his natural-born talent to both his parents—but mostly to his mother, who was said to possess considerable talent. She played piano and taught herself to play Hawaiian-style guitar, with moves that Jack often emulated, especially when he was learning to play the instrument. She was also said to have had an extraordinary singing voice.

Faced with tough economic hardships, the Snows struggled to make ends meet. George, a trained millwright, had to take jobs throughout Nova Scotia, New Brunswick, and the State of Maine. Travelling for work was not easy for him, as it meant he didn't see much of his children, but a man had to provide for his family even if it meant leaving them for long periods of time. When Jack was six years of age, his father took a job at a wholesale grocery store in Halifax. While it was closer to Brooklyn, the job still took George away from home throughout the week and away from his family when they needed him most. However, even though the journey was tedious, George would ride the train from Halifax to Brooklyn every Friday and then back again on Sunday so that he could be with his family for a few days. (This was at a time when the train was the common mode of transportation in Nova Scotia. Motor vehicles were few and roads were nothing more than gravel paths, often impassible, especially in bad weather.)

Undated photo of Hank Snow's father, George Lewis Snow. The woman in the photo is believed to be Hank's grandmother Godfrey.

During these difficult times, there was no place for pride, and Marie did whatever she had to do to provide for her children. To help out with expenses, she took work wherever she could find it, and often ended up doing chores for the wealthy families in the community, cleaning houses to earn a few dollars. Marie told her children it was honest work and that it was nothing to be ashamed of. She would explain that life sometimes provided opportunities in the most unlikely of places if one was willing make the most of them, a lesson Jack took to heart and drew upon throughout his lifetime.

Jack's grandmother on his father's side, Peninah Jane (Anthony), lived a short distance from the Snow's modest home in Brooklyn. Peninah Jane and William Lewis Reeves Snow had only one son, George. After William died at age twenty-three in 1888, Peninah married Curtis Godfrey and the couple lived in Brooklyn. For reasons that were never fully explained to Jack, his grandmother Godfrey did not get along well with Marie, and the children were not permitted to have much contact with the older woman, a directive that seemed cruel at first to Jack considering the woman was his grandmother. However, Jack did like spending time with his step-grandfather, Curtis Godfrey, whenever possible. Even though it meant defying his mother's wishes and sneaking away from his own home on occasion, Jack spent many memorable days helping the aging man do chores around the yard and milking the cow, which was more like a family pet than a food source. Despite his small stature, which made physical work difficult, Jack especially enjoyed helping his step-grandfather mow hay in the summer and then store it in the barn loft, not easy for a boy under the age of seven. Forever cognizant of his mother's directive, Jack did his best to keep his distance from his grandmother during these visits.

Despite the ongoing economic difficulties that found the family in such oppressive poverty, life in the Snow home was typical of most households of the era: they were forced to scrounge for food, stretch their few resources, and to take whatever jobs they could find. However, by the time Jack was six or seven, things took a turn for the worse. His parents began experiencing marital problems, perhaps brought on by the separation caused by his father being away for work, which left his mother to cope with raising four children on very little money. Or perhaps it was brought about by the escalating tension between Jack's mother and grandmother. Whatever the reason, the situation deteriorated until the stress tore the family apart. As the Snows' marital problems intensified, whatever happiness had previously existed in the household all but dissipated, as fears of an impending separation intensified. This continued for a time, until one day the inevitable happened.

The day his father left was particularly difficult for Jack, and left emotional scars he would carry for his entire life. In his autobiography, *The Hank Snow Story*, published in 1994 by the University of Illinois Press, Snow wrote on the subject:

> I'll never forget the day my dad left home. I can remember it as if it was yesterday. He borrowed a small four-wheel cart from my step-grandfather Godfrey, and I helped Dad load his trunk on the wagon. As I was

pulling the wagon down to the train station about a mile away, Dad didn't say a word and I was wondering where he was going and if he would ever come back. At the station he patted me on the back and gave me a nickel. I remember his exact words: "Well, good-bye, son. I may see you again, and I may never see you again." Dad boarded the train and waved good-bye.

This was one of many tough life lessons that Jack would learn over the next few years. Another came when the court approved a legal separation between his parents. But the hardest was yet to come. In 1922 the courts ruled that, because of financial reasons, Marie could no longer keep any of her children. They felt that, because of her economic situation, she could not adequately provide for them. Jack, who was around eight at the time, went to live in his grandmother Godfrey's house with the woman he had previously been warned to avoid. His sisters, Nina and Marion, were placed in separate foster homes, while Lillian, the oldest at age sixteen, went to live with her Aunt Cecile— one of Marie's three sisters—in Stewiacke, Colchester County.

It was hard for young Jack to comprehend what had happened. It seemed one minute his had been a happy family struggling to get by and the next they had been torn apart and scattered in the wind. The Snows hadn't had much by way of material things, but before the divorce at least the family had had each other. In just a few short months, Jack's world had fallen apart and his worst nightmares had become a reality.

Additional hardships were to follow as young Jack quickly came to understand why his mother had so despised his grandmother. It started on the day he moved in, when she warned him against using his mother's name in her presence. "Never mention Marie in the house," she warned the young boy, and from day one he was forbidden to ever have any contact with his mother, or he would be severely punished.

Later in life, Jack would often admit that he had been terrified of his grandmother and had believed she would make good on her threats to punish him if he disobeyed her. In fact, she did just that on many occasions. In talking about his grandmother Godfrey, he often said, "The woman scared the hell out of me."

He had good reason to be scared.

Discipline is one thing, but Jack's grandmother was strict beyond reason. She required that he complete a list of chores to her exact satisfaction and if he didn't do as she demanded, he would be severely punished. He suffered often, as nothing he did ever suited her. She would accept no excuses or explanations, and her punishments varied from stern lectures, which included ridiculing him for being "worthless" and "useless," to keeping him inside the house away from his friends, even in the high heat of summer, and locking him in his small, closet-like room for several hours at a time during which he had no contact with anyone else. On many occasions she deprived him of his meals, and then there were the lashings he endured and often described as "brutal."

It's clear that, as far as Jack was concerned, his grandmother was a complete and utter tyrant in that house, so much so that she was even feared by the boy's step-grandfather. Her verbal assaults were constant and demeaning, her demands of the old man unreasonable. Many times, Snow would recall later on, he had witnessed his grandmother beat her husband over the head with a broom handle. In fact, his step-grandfather feared her so profoundly that he often stayed away from the house, choosing instead to sleep in the cold woods with no warm clothes or food to eat. Jack recalled that his step-grandfather would be out there for days at a time, until his grandmother sent some of the neighbourhood men to bring him home. While Jack understood the old man's need to run away, the downside of his step-grandfather's escapes was that his grandmother took her anger out on him.

As a result of living in constant fear, Jack developed a bedwetting problem, the rate of which increased with his anxiety. And the more it happened, the less forgiving and the more hateful his grandmother became. Every morning when Jack got out of bed, grandmother Godfrey would immediately turn back the covers to see if the blankets were wet. If they were, she'd beat him with a leather strap, insisting that he stop his "dirty" habit. But Jack's anxiety only deepened with each beating, which, in turn, made him wet the bed even more. It was a vicious cycle.

Later in life, when Hank Snow began speaking out about the horrors of child abuse, he encouraged parents to see bedwetting as a sign of deeper psychological problems, and a cry for help. Beating a child in such emotional turmoil would not help correct the problem, he said, but would only make it worse. Snow claimed that with love and support and understanding, a child would outgrow the habit. Eventually, Jack was able to control his bedwetting, but it was certainly not thanks to any help from his grandmother.

These were dark times for Clarence "Jack" Snow. Separated from his mother and desperately missing his father and sisters, his emotions hit rock bottom. With no contact with his family, he felt alone, isolated, and lost; cut off from anyone who might care for him. As an adult talking about his rough childhood, Snow admitted that he could never remember a time when his grandmother showed any tenderness toward him. Even though he had been a young child facing the breakup of his family, she never once hugged him, complimented him, or had a kind word to say to him. Not ever.

Things changed about a year and a half after Jack went to live with his grandmother. One day, a classmate came to Jack in the schoolyard and told him that Jack's mother was waiting up the road to see him; she had brought a gift for him. Until that time, Jack had not known his mother's whereabouts or if she was even still alive. They had to keep their meeting a secret, as Jack feared his grandmother would punish him if she knew they had met. Jack kept his mother's gift—a brown leather belt with a silver buckle—well hidden for fear that if his grandmother saw it, she would know he had seen his mother contrary to her wishes and would take it away from him. At a time when the young Jack felt so alone, the cherished belt and buckle became an important link to his mother.

Eventually, Jack discovered that his mother had found a job in Liverpool, working as a live-in housekeeper for an older gentleman who operated a livery in town. Even though his mother had warned Jack not to come to Liverpool to see her, worried that the authorities—and his grandmother—would find out, he threw caution to the wind. He was willing to defy his grandmother and risk his own well-being to see his mother.

Despite his fear of being discovered, by the summer of 1925 Jack was visiting Liverpool more frequently. He'd often follow the Canadian National Rail line from Brooklyn to get to his destination, about half an hour to forty minutes by foot. Eventually, the trips to see his mother became so important to Jack that he'd risk not having a place to sleep at night when he got to Liverpool or when he returned to his grandmother's house. (He would often find the front door locked and the lights turned off when he got back to Brooklyn.) He spent many cold and wet nights sleeping in cellars, barns, and even under bushes, basically anywhere he could lay his head. Often, on cold nights, he would walk to the tiny railroad station in Liverpool, where it was warm. There, he'd sleep on the benches, out of the elements. (This is the same station that today houses the Hank Snow Home Town Museum.)

No matter what he had to do, and despite what his grandmother told him, Jack never stopped believing that his mother loved him very much and that someday, somehow, he would go live with her again. In fact, it was Jack's dream that his whole family would eventually be reunited; that his mother, his sisters, and he would live together again. Of course, his grandmother did everything she could to prevent any such thing from happening.

Although Jack's grandmother never outwardly asked about his increased trips to Liverpool, he believed that she had somehow learned about his ongoing meetings with his mother. In response, she turned up the abuse: locking him in his room, keeping him away from other children, physically beating him, and verbally berating his mother. His grandmother even petitioned the courts to take him away to reform school, but it was no good. If anything, Jack felt his grandmother's evil ways made him more determined to reunite with his mother. Finally, despite his grandmother's relentless efforts to keep Jack and his mother apart, the courts ruled that it was best for Jack to live with Marie and eventually cleared the way for him to move in with his mother, who was still working in Liverpool as a live-in housekeeper.

Within a few short months, however, fate conspired against the family once again as his mother's employer's health faded, and her job came to an end. The house in which Jack and his mother were staying was sold and they were forced to move out, leaving them homeless.

By this time, Jack's oldest sister, Lillian, had met and married Wilbert Risser, a local fisherman from Lunenburg, another fishing

The historic CN train station in Liverpool where Jack spent many nights as a young boy after running away from his grandmother's home in Brooklyn to see his mother in Liverpool.

town further down the coast. The couple didn't have much room, but Lillian invited Jack and their mother to move into their small, square home located in a tiny settlement called Black Rocks, more commonly known today as Stonehurst. Jack later described the crumbly, old, five-room home perched high atop a cliff as the coldest house he'd ever lived in. There he slept on a broken-down couch with exposed coil springs. It wasn't that his sister treated him badly. In fact, just the opposite was true. She just didn't have the money to purchase him a bed, so he had to make do. Jack was in no position to complain, though, and he was grateful to have a roof over his head. And after what he had gone through with his grandmother, he was forever thankful to be reunited with members of his immediate family.

But it wasn't long after Jack, his mother, his sister, and her husband moved in together that it became clear that Jack's new brother-in-law, Wilbert, did not want him around the house. In short order, Wilbert began verbally abusing Jack and his mother, calling them names, and complaining about having more mouths to feed. He gave Jack a particularly difficult time, even though he and his mother were there on Lillian's invitation. Despite Jack's efforts to help out—daily chores that included cutting firewood and washing the house's wooden floors—nothing was good enough for Wilbert. He'd often unleash his anger on Jack, who was still trying to recover from the abuse he had suffered at the hands of his grandmother.

Even though Jack and his mother continued to live with Lillian and Wilbert, the situation grew increasingly worse for the young boy. But it became especially bad for Jack when his mother became interested in, and then eventually married, Wilbert's friend and fishing partner, Charles Enos Tanner. Jack could never understand what his mother saw in Charlie Tanner, and although he wanted her to be happy again, for Jack, happiness was an elusive thing; it seemed he would go from one bad situation to an even worse one. When talking about his stepfather, he'd always say: "It was hate at first sight."

Charlie's verbal barbs were unrelenting and eventually the abuse became physical, with Charlie sometimes turning on young Jack without provocation or warning. Eventually, Jack concluded that Charlie's intense hatred toward him stemmed form a deep-rooted jealousy that grew from his mother's affection toward her own son. In talking about this time in his life, Snow would often say that he couldn't understand how someone as caring and loving as his mother could have fallen for such a hateful man. But it was clear that she had feelings for Charlie and Jack was forced to adapt, even if it meant enduring things that no young boy should ever have to face.

Snow admitted later in life that as Charlie's verbal berating became constant, there were times when he actually wished he was back living with his grandmother. That was a lot of hate for a twelve-year-old child to carry around. Though he was young and physically small, Jack came to believe that if he could find work and earn money to pay for his board, maybe things would get better for him. Maybe, he hoped, Charlie would take it easier on him. But like everywhere else in the world at that time, Canada was in the throes of a deep economic depression. Employment opportunities were scarce and whatever jobs were available were quickly filled by able-bodied men who were more capable of doing the work than Jack, an eighty-pound kid prone to sickness.

At this point in Jack's life, his mother had mail-ordered a Hawaiian guitar and several songbooks. Jack was delighted when the

Marie Alice Snow with her prized guitar, the first instrument Jack learned to play.

instrument arrived and, while he didn't know it yet, his mother's decision to purchase it marked a turning point in his life. Jack would sit for
hours, listening as she strummed. He was amazed at the sound of her
voice as she sang along. Sometimes he'd sing along as well, and in time
she allowed him to play that guitar, introducing him to the instrument
that would become a major part of his life. At a time when there wasn't

much happiness in Jack's life, his mother's praise meant a great deal to him. He drank it in when she gushed at his natural "God-given talent," and told him that someday he would become a professional singer and guitar player. How prophetic her words truly were.

Eventually, as Jack's skills improved, his mother allowed him to play the guitar for neighbours who also heaped compliments upon him. Although such praise was foreign to Jack at that stage in his life, the positive remarks he received following those performances stayed with him for the rest of his life; they remained as important to him as the legions of fans who would someday buy his records and line up to attend his concerts. Throughout his life, Jack always credited his mother's mail-order guitar for kick-starting his interest in music.

"God bless her," Snow would often say fondly when talking about his beloved mother, for he believed that while she claimed it was for herself, she may have actually bought the guitar for him as a way of helping him cope with his living conditions.

Off to Sea

Despite Jack's best efforts to avoid strife in his sister's home, he felt that both Charlie Tanner and Wilbert Risser had it out for him. He had no idea why they would treat him so badly, other than the clear fact that they simply did not want him around. He was grateful to have somewhere to lay his head out of the elements, but the men's aggressive behaviour was hard on him. But, as luck would have it, right around this time he heard about an employment opportunity on board one of the fishing schooners sailing out of Lunenburg.

A traditional fishing schooner carried a crew of twenty-two men, plus a flunky, or cabin boy, who did a variety of jobs for the cook and captain but was not paid. However, when not carrying out his regular duties, a flunky could fish from the ship on his own time and sell his catch once the vessel arrived back in port, an effort that could result in a significant payday. Additionally, the job offered several hearty meals a day and a warm, clean bed, almost as good as a paycheque in those days.

Although Jack had never been to sea, he desperately wanted the job. It would allow him to escape the tiny house and the abuse he endured there. Initially, he feared his physical stature and sickly appearance might be a problem, but in the spring of 1926, at the age of twelve, Jack Snow went to sea as a ship's flunky, landing his first job in the fishing industry on board the *Grace Boehner*, a 120-foot-long schooner. Powered by sail, the vessel used kerosene lamps for light— there were no such things as generators in those days. Admittedly, Jack was intimidated by the job. Growing up near the ocean, he was aware of the dangers that come with working on the fishing boats, but he felt he had no alternative. He also saw the opportunity as an adventure, and hoped the job would prove his worth to his tormentors once and for all.

Captained by Lapene Crouse, the *Grace Boehner* could reach a maximum speed of twelve to fourteen knots in a strong wind. The schooner, crewed mostly by men from Nova Scotia and Newfoundland, fished on the Western and Grand Banks of the North Atlantic, with catches consisting mostly of codfish, haddock, and halibut, all of which were plentiful a century ago. For the next four years Jack worked on various fishing vessels, first as a flunky and then eventually in other positions—such as throater, the guy on the boat who cut the throats of the codfish and then passed them along to the next guy, who gutted them—that paid full wages. He often admitted that working on the fishing boats was hard for a boy of his age and stature, but he stuck it out, turning over most of his wages to Charlie Tanner to help cover his living expenses. He had hoped the money might reduce the amount of abuse he suffered in the home. Sadly, he was wrong.

From that first trip on board the *Grace Boehner*, Jack earned $24.65, and with the few dollars he kept for himself after paying Charlie for room and board, he purchased clothing and shoes, which he desperately needed. (He often told the story of being so poor that he would sometimes put several layers of cardboard inside his shoes to cover the holes in the soles. The cardboard patches wouldn't last if he had to walk any great distance or if they got wet, and it wasn't long before Jack would be walking on human leather again.) But no matter what he did or how much he contributed to the household, it was never sufficient. It was clear to Jack that Charlie simply did not like him, and the turmoil at home continued. If Jack had had any other alternative, he would have simply moved out of the house, but he had nowhere else to go.

However, not everything in Jack Snow's young life was dark and desperate. When he returned home following this first fishing trip, he was delighted to find that his mother had scraped up two dollars to buy an old Victrola gramophone and two records, *The Wreck of the Old '97* and *The Prisoner's Song*, by Vernon Dalhart, a popular American singer and songwriter from the early 1900s who was considered a major influence on early country music. It was through those records that Jack found his escape. As he listened to those songs over and over, inspired by the simple but meaningful lyrics and the basic instrumentation, Jack told himself he wanted to make records just like that man from Texas someday.

After practising the guitar for several months, Jack felt he was ready to perform in front of others. During leisure time on board the fishing schooners he would sometimes sing for the crew and, occasionally, even perform a few simple dance steps he had created. The reaction was positive and the crew would applaud, praise, and encourage Jack, telling him that he had a fine singing voice—good enough to be on the radio. That positive reinforcement was more valuable to Jack than any amount of money he received from his job. He later said that praise from his fellow crewmen was worth a million dollars, and it went a long way in building his confidence—positive reinforcement that he desperately needed. Years down the road, when the going got tough, he would remember those compliments and draw upon them for the courage to pursue his dreams. He recognized that his early efforts were all part of making him the person and performer that he eventually became.

Following his second fishing trip, and again after giving much of his pay to Charlie, Jack purchased his first guitar, a $5.95 T. Eaton Special, through a mail-order catalogue. The instrument may not have been much to brag about, but it was his, paid for with money he'd earned, and Jack was proud of that. With practise, he learned basic chords and in time he was strumming the little guitar like a pro. He cherished that instrument as if it were the most expensive guitar in Canada.

Although the music he made with that guitar always offered him a brief reprieve, it could not block out the abuse and ridicule Jack continued to suffer at the hands of his stepfather. In fact, between fishing trips he often found himself with nowhere to live. To avoid confrontation, Jack would sometimes stay with other family members, such as his grandmother Boutlier—his mother's mother—who lived in Western Head, a tiny coastal hamlet near Liverpool. Unlike his grandmother Godfrey, who he now only saw on rare occasions, he enjoyed seeing his maternal grandmother. Sometimes Jack went to live with his second-oldest sister, Nina, and her husband, Ritchie Tanner (no relation to Charlie Tanner), in Halifax. He and Ritchie often sailed on the same fishing boats—Ritchie taught him a great deal about the work—and they got along well.

In Halifax, Ritchie managed to get Jack a job at the same fish-processing plant where he worked between fishing trips. But Jack was fired after the first week because he couldn't lift the heavy boxes full of fish. From there, Jack took to selling the *Halifax Herald*, the city's daily newspaper, on the street. When he failed to sell any, he quit. Next he lucked into a job at Fader's Pharmacy, located at 135 Hollis Street on the corner of Sackville Street, making three dollars a week delivering prescriptions and other personal care items to customers. He kept this job until the spring of 1927, when he returned to Lunenburg and went fishing aboard the *Gilbert B. Walters* under the command of Captain Sonny Walters.

Over the next few years, Jack sailed several trips on the *Gilbert B. Walters*. When he wasn't working, he'd listen to the ship's radio, a rare luxury in the 1920s. Throughout 1927 and 1928 he listened to artists like Vernon Dalhart and Carson Robison, and when entertaining the crew he would attempt to emulate their sound. As before, his efforts earned him much applause and encouragement from the other men to pursue a career in music, praise that Jack was now beginning to take seriously. The idea of making records and being heard on the radio did sound appealing to Jack, but for now he had to focus on surviving in the harsh world that, up to that point, had not been kind to him.

Life as a fisherman on the often-tumultuous Atlantic Ocean isn't easy at the best of times, and on rough seas it can be one of the worst nightmares imaginable. Jack often talked about the brush with death that led him to make a life-altering decision. He openly wondered what his life would have been like if not for the incident that finally convinced him that a fisherman's life was not for him.

In August 1930, Jack took his last trip to sea, aboard another Lunenburg-based schooner, the *Maxwell F. Corkum*, captained by Leo Corkum. Late summer and early fall is traditionally the time of year when major storms brew in the North Atlantic, and throughout their storied histories, the seafaring communities along Nova Scotia's South Shore have had many brushes with disaster. With strong winds and seas sometimes peaking as high as twenty-storey buildings, such storms, experienced aboard a schooner, can be a harrowing experience; they can bring even the hardiest man to his knees.

As these powerful storms blow across the region, they often leave a trail of death and destruction in their wake. To experience such fury first-hand—with waves so powerful that they tossed the boat around as though it were a toy—led to an epiphany for Jack. With news of the devastating August Gales from the previous two years still fresh in the minds of most fishermen in the region, Jack ultimately concluded that he could not devote his entire life to the fishery. While he was thankful for the job and welcomed the money he had earned, he knew he was just not cut out for that kind of work. When the battered schooner eventually limped into the port of Canso, Cape Breton, in the late summer of 1930, he disembarked and never returned. Despite the regular paycheque he desperately needed, Jack vowed that he was done on the fishing boats.

At age sixteen, after four years working on the schooners, Jack's career on the sea had come to a resounding halt. While he'd sometimes entertain the idea of returning to the sea when things got particularly tough in future years, he always dismissed the notion, thinking he just wouldn't be able to handle it, mentally or physically. Whenever he thought of those massive waves crashing over the ship's bow, fuelled by hurricane-force winds, he knew there was no way he could ever go back sea. Life may have been tough for him at times but he reasoned that at least he was safe, and would remain safe, with his feet planted firmly on the ground.

Of course, leaving the sea behind meant that Jack now had to find some other way to earn money. He was homeless, floating between family members and staying for short periods until he felt he had outstayed his welcome. Although Jack knew his mother would welcome him back if he wanted to come live with her, he also knew that Charlie Tanner would not easily accept him again. He was homeless, penniless, unemployed, and desperate; adrift on a sea of poverty and hopelessness, he wandered aimlessly about town and slept wherever he could.

Even though times were exceptionally tough for everyone during the Depression, Nina and Ritchie, who by this time had moved back to Lunenburg to be close to the fishing fleet, again convinced Jack to come stay with them. Although Ritchie was now unemployed and Jack knew it would not be easy for the couple to have another mouth to feed, he reluctantly accepted their generous offer. He really had no other option.

With the little money he had managed to save from his last fishing trip, and with Ritchie's help, Jack purchased a .22 rifle. His father had taught him to shoot many years earlier in Brooklyn, so he still had the skill even thought he hadn't fired a gun in many years. With the .22, Jack hunted rabbits and other small game in the local woods, which gave him, Ritchie, and Nina meat in the winter, and made him feel like a contributor to the household. He also tried selling the extra rabbits door to door, but had little luck; others were facing the same economic woes and were doing the same thing.

Desperate for money and unable to find a job in the area, Jack, at age sixteen, became a bootlegger. This was the era of Prohibition in Canada, when the possession of alcohol was illegal and getting caught with it, let alone selling it, had serious consequences, especially for someone so young. But in an effort to acquire cash, Jack purchased contraband rum that had been smuggled into Stonehurst by boat operators known as "rum-runners," and then tried to resell it for a small markup. (Bootleggers made their profits by watering down the undiluted two hundred-proof rum and reselling it.) This career was short-lived for Jack, however. He tried selling one batch, but the venture proved unprofitable and his guilty conscience got the best of him. He admitted that he could not stop thinking about how disappointed his mother would be if she discovered he was making money on the black market, especially from selling contraband liquor.

Between jobs, Jack would often venture into the many picturesque villages and wharves that surround the Town of Lunenburg. One of his favourite areas to visit was Blue Rocks, a popular destination on the South Shore for Canadian and American tourists, among them artists who came to capture the natural beauty on canvas. It was there that Jack honed his considerable skills as a painter. In time, he became quite renowned for

An undated picture of a young Hank Snow sitting on a railing. Location unknown.

his paintings—but while the hobby helped to fill his time and relieve his stress, his artistic talents didn't pay him anything and he was still desperate for employment.

Jack's need for a job became even more urgent when he saw an advertisement in the T. Eaton catalogue for a guitar that he "just had to have," as he often recounted. It cost $12.95, a fortune to him at the time. With no money and few job prospects in Lunenburg, he devised a plan to raise the necessary funds: he sold his T. Eaton Special for $5 and earned the remaining $7.95 painting the wooden spokes on the wheels of a new car that a local businessman had recently purchased. It wasn't exactly art, but the assignment paid his fee. In the end, he mused, his painting talent *did* pay off for him. After raising the money, Jack mail-ordered the guitar and waited impatiently for its arrival.

With his new guitar in hand, Jack devoted most of his free time to learning new songs, mostly those by country music legend Jimmie Rodgers, who by then had become his idol. He vowed that someday he wanted "to be just like him." From the first time he heard the Rodgers classic, "Moonlight and Skies" on the ship's radio, he emulated the singer's sound and style, thinking these techniques would be his ticket to getting on the radio just like his idol.

It didn't take long for word about this budding entertainer who could play the guitar and sing country music to spread around the small community of Lunenburg. Before long, with the help of Nina and Ritchie, Jack was being invited to perform for neighbours and friends around town, all the while dreaming about someday getting on CHNS, a Halifax radio station based at the Lord Nelson Hotel that broadcast country music.

Years later, in his autobiography, Jack wrote about that dream: "On the back scribbler cover I drew a picture of a record and microphone at radio station CHNS. The title of the song on the record was 'My Blue-Eyed Jane,' by Clarence E. Snow. Of course, this was a Jimmie Rodgers song, but eventually, when my dreams came true, I recorded the song Hank Snow style."

News of the young singer and guitar player from Lunenburg soon reached other communities. Eventually Jack was invited by the organizers of a charity show to perform for the first time, at the age of sixteen, in front of a live audience in the neighbouring town of Bridgewater. "This was a happy moment for me," he wrote in his book. "Somebody besides family thought I had talent as a singer. I was walking on air." At the show, he performed an old tune he had been practising called "I Went to See My Gal Last Night" and received a standing ovation. He basked in the applause, but the reality of his life soon cut the celebration short. He needed a job, desperately.

Feeling that he had outlived his stay at Nina and Ritchie's, Jack went to live with his oldest sister, Lillian, and Wilbert Risser in Stonehurst. Not wanting to impose on them for fear of inciting Wilbert's wrath, Jack would go into Lunenburg searching for work. Eventually, he heard of a job opening up in a livery stable owned by Solly Knickle. Described as a "nice old man" by those who knew him, Solly saw something in the frail young Jack and he hired him right on the spot. This was Jack's introduction to horses, and he knew immediately that he loved working with them. For six dollars a week, the job required him to groom and help take care of six horses as well as clean the stables, all chores that he liked to do. He also earned his pay by transporting passengers and freight to and from the train station. "This turned out to be one of the most enjoyable jobs I have ever had," he often said. But, unfortunately, it, like so many of his jobs, was short-lived.

Knickle died, and less than a year later the stables and horses were sold, throwing Jack out of work yet again. He quickly landed another job in a local meat market for six dollars a week, but soon afterwards the store closed due to a lack of business. The Depression had made finding steady employment virtually impossible and competition from hundreds of others looking for work meant the job prospects were bleak.

Jack tried as hard as he could to become self-sufficient, but had little luck. Continuing to bounce from the home of one family member to the next, he took on a number of jobs wherever he could find them. He unloaded salt from the three-mast, square-rigged ships at the Lunenburg wharf for fifteen cents an hour. He tried selling silverware, men's wristwatches, hand cleaner, and fish door to door, but with little luck. It soon became obvious to him that he just was not a salesman. When those ventures failed, Jack made his way back to the wharves and got a job unloading coal from big steamers. It was probably the hardest and dirtiest work he ever had to do, but he knew he could not afford to be picky. It was now 1931, the Depression had deepened, Jack was seventeen, and he was more desperate than ever. By this time, he was literally wearing rags on his back and so, like many others from this bleak time, he swallowed his pride and went door to door asking housewives if they had any old clothes to donate to charity. He didn't tell them that he was the charity in question.

Jumping at any opportunity that came along, Jack joined the militia unit stationed in Lunenburg at the time, training one night a week for several months. The government paid him a lump sum of twelve dollars at the end of the training, but it was hardly enough to live on. The following January, out of the blue, Jack's stepfather Charlie offered to take him scallop raking, for which he earned a dollar a day. Although somewhat leery of Charlie's motives, Jack took up the offer and worked with him until the end of the scalloping season that spring. From there, Jack landed a job packing and drying fish at the Adams and Knickle fish-processing plant on the Lunenburg waterfront.

Around this same time, Jack received an unexpected letter from his father, who he hadn't seen or heard from in almost ten years. In the letter, Jack learned his father was now living in a small settlement called Pleasantville, located about thirty-seven kilometres inland from Lunenburg. He had married a widow, Fanny Blakney, who had three children from her first marriage, and had also had a child with her, a girl named Ethel. Jack's father invited him to come live with him and Jack was happy to take up the offer. Hoping her son would finally reconnect with his father, Jack's mother gave him the few cents for the train ride from Lunenburg to Bridgewater, where his father was waiting for him. It was a happy reunion.

In Pleasantville, Jack learned that his father had actually been doing fairly well in the years since he'd left his struggling family in Brooklyn. When he'd married Fanny, the senior Snow had also acquired her small farm and many hectares of timber, which he was harvesting and selling to the local sawmills for a reasonable profit. Jack stayed with his father for several months, helping to cut pulpwood. While he was excited to get reacquainted with his father after all those years, like always, the longing to be near his mother pulled him back to Lunenburg. In December 1931, Jack left Pleasantville and made his way back to the coast.

Chasing a Dream

Jack hadn't seen his mother in several months, and he was anxious to reconnect with her. Although apprehensive about his stepfather's potential reaction, Jack hitchhiked the thirty-seven kilometres from Pleasantville back to his mother's house in Lunenburg along with his stepbrother, Ray—one of Fanny's children from her earlier marriage—who had also been helping on the woodlot.

It was Christmas Eve 1931 when the boys arrived back in Lunenburg. Jack was enjoying a wonderful reunion with his mother until Charlie arrived home. He was not happy to find the visitors in his house, and, following an exchange of angry words, Jack and Ray quickly fled. Fearing for their safety, they reported the incident to the town's chief of police, who responded by telling them there was nothing the authorities could do unless Charlie caused them bodily harm, which Jack always reasoned would have been too little, too late.

Although he was disappointed he didn't have more time with his mother during that visit, there was no way Jack could have risked going back to see her. With nowhere to go and no intention of returning to the house, Jack and Ray hung around the Lunenburg post office for the rest of the night. The next morning, in the bitter cold, they hitchhiked back to Pleasantville. Jack stayed with the family and worked in his father's woodlot until the following spring, at which time he returned to Lunenburg and moved back in with Nina and Ritchie. He now avoided Charlie as much as possible.

Around the same time, Jack's mother, Marie, received an invitation from her sister Grace, asking her to come back to Brooklyn. Marie took the offer and moved there to live with Grace and her family. Charlie, on the other hand, would remain in Lunenburg until Marie sent word that she was settled. A few weeks after their mother left, Jack and his younger sister, Marion, followed Marie back to the little village where they were born, hitching rides on the pulpwood trucks heading to the pulp and paper mill.

Times weren't any easier for the family in Brooklyn, not that Jack had really expected them to be. The few dollars their mother had somehow managed to save quickly disappeared, and Charlie was unable to find work there. The family was destitute and living in extreme poverty. There was no food in the house. With the hope of raising money to at least buy household staples, their mother had Jack and Marion go door to door in Liverpool trying to sell raffle tickets for her Hawaiian guitar, but they had no luck. Money was scarce for everyone, and what few cents people had couldn't be squandered on the chance to win a musical instrument. As hungry as he was, Jack was secretly relieved about this failure: he didn't want his mother to have to give up the guitar she loved so much.

These were not happy times. With Charlie now living in Brooklyn and making life miserable for the young man, Jack and Marion decided to head back to be with their sister Nina in Lunenburg, where Jack at least felt welcome. In the middle of February, with snow covering the ground, Jack and Marion dressed in their meagre clothing and headed for Nina's house, hoping to make it before they froze to death. On the first night they made it to Mill Village, a small settlement hugging the banks of the Medway River, some fifteen kilometres from Brooklyn. There, cold and hungry, Jack and his sister knocked on the door of the first house they came across. Jack never forgot the nice woman who took them, two strangers, into her home, gave them food and a warm place to sleep for the night.

The next morning, following a hearty breakfast generously supplied by the nice woman, Jack and Marion continued their journey to Lunenburg, where they remained with Nina and her husband until 1933. While in Lunenburg, Jack also spent a great deal of time with his other sister, Lillian. Her husband, Wilbert, completely ignored him, but that was okay with Jack. He found solace by getting lost in his sister's collection of Jimmie Rodgers records.

As Jack listened to Rodgers, he decided that he could learn to play music like that, and he practised every chance he had, playing his $12.95 guitar and learning the lyrics to every Rodgers song on those records. The more he listened, the more determined he was to become a successful entertainer. He vowed to let nothing stand in his way.

Jack knew that making it in the entertainment industry wouldn't be easy, especially during the Depression, when music was nothing more than an afterthought for most people. Still, by 1933, Jack had decided that if he was going to make it in the music business, then he had to go to Halifax and somehow get on CHNS. Determined to make his dreams a reality, in early March 1933, he wrote to the managing director of the country music station asking for an audition. Later that same month he received a reply addressed to Mr. Clarence E. Snow:

March 14, 1933

Dear Mr. Snow:

We have your letter and I regret to tell you that we are
not able to offer you anything at this station. All the
artists who appear here are paid by the sponsors of the
programs and unless a sponsor was to ask for you, we
could not do anything for you. If, however, your services are required, we have your name on file.

Yours very truly,

William Coates Borrett
Managing Director

Though some might consider this letter to be a rejection, Jack was
impressed that the station's managing director had taken time from
his busy schedule to write him personally. As Jack saw it, the letter
didn't exactly say for him *not* to come to Halifax. Spurred on, he
made up his mind to rise above the suffocating poverty that had consumed him and his family his entire life. He vowed that despite the
seemingly insurmountable odds, he was going to make something of
himself and he would let nothing—certainly not a polite letter from
a station manager—stand in his way.

May 9, 1933, was a day that changed Jack's life. Empowered by
Borrett's response, he decided that the time had come for him to head
to Halifax, even if he had to bring Marion with him; he had no intention
of leaving her to fend for herself. Before he could go, though, he needed
money, which meant that he once again had to find a job. He was so
desperate for work that he even considered going back to the schooners
for another trip, but he didn't think he could handle the stress.

As luck would have it, Jack's situation didn't get to that point.
One morning, while hanging around the Lunenburg waterfront, Jack
heard that two men were looking for someone to scrape and repaint
the deck, cabin, and wheelhouse of an old schooner they had recently
purchased. He stepped up and they hired him right on the spot. The

work lasted three weeks and for his efforts he earned $32.50, not a great deal of money even in those days, but surely enough to take him and Marion to Halifax. With their few belongings stuffed in an old suitcase held together with a piece of rope and his guitar in hand, Jack and his sister headed down the dusty dirt road to whatever fate awaited them in the big city.

Once in Halifax, the duo made their way to the tiny community of Fairview on the city's outskirts, where they located the home of the daughter of a "nice old woman" Jack had known in Lunenburg. The woman had always told him that if he was ever in Halifax, he should look up her daughter, and so here he was. The family immediately took the pair into their home, inviting them to stay as long as they wanted. It was a generous offer, and one that Jack would never forget. If they hadn't been invited to stay there, he and Marion would have had no other place to go.

After moving into the Fairview house, Jack immediately contacted CHNS and, to his surprise, was given an appointment to meet with the managing director. But fate had other plans for him. The next afternoon, dressed in the best clothes he had, Jack made his way to the Lord Nelson and up to the seventh floor, where he was introduced to Cecil Landry, the station's chief engineer and announcer, who gave him his audition right then and there. Jack wasn't at all nervous, even though the studio and recording instruments were all new to him—and despite the fact that he had not been prepared to perform. But, like Jack would do many times throughout his lifetime, he took advantage of the opportunity, realizing that such chances come along once, maybe twice, if you're lucky.

For his audition, Jack sang "A Letter From Home Sweet Home" followed by a Jimmie Rodgers song. He finished his audition by yodeling, a skill he had been practising for many years, especially while on the boats. He made a good first impression.

In his autobiography, Snow wrote about Landry's reaction that day: "'That was pretty good. You have a good voice and you play your guitar pretty well, too.'" He then told Jack to go home and think of a theme song. He would be going on the air that night at seven o'clock for fifteen minutes. Clarence Eugene "Jack" Snow was finally on his way.

"Hank" Snow is Born

Things were happening even more quickly than Jack Snow could have imagined or dared to hope for. During that first broadcast he made sure to sing "My Blue-Eyed Jane," just as he had always dreamed of doing. That same afternoon, influenced by his idol, Jimmie Rodgers, Jack wrote his show's theme song, "The Yodeling Cowboy."

> At the set of the sun when my work is done
> On my pony I take a ride
> Where the varmints prowl and the coyotes howl,
> With my .44 on my side.

At the conclusion of the show he finished the song with these lyrics.

> I go down that lonesome trail,
> Just galloping along.
> I love to sing this yodeling cowboy song.

Then he ended with a yodel.

Four days after his first show aired on CHNS, Jack was called back to pick up his fan mail and was shocked to discover the station had received almost ninety letters addressed to "Clarence Snow." Several days later, he received another surprise when he saw an advertisement in the paper listing the station's programs. The listing for Saturday evening's seven o'clock time slot read, "Clarence Snow and his Guitar." It was an amazing feeling, he said, to see his name in print promoting his show.

Of all the people Jack met throughout his life, he largely credited Cecil Landry—who remained a close friend until Cecil's death—for giving him his first big break in the music business. Landry encouraged Jack and taught him important skills about entertaining that he would often call upon throughout his career. In fact, Landry was the first person to ever record Jack's voice, on aluminum discs at the CHNS station. Jack sang the traditional standards, "Old Faithful" and "The Old Rugged Cross."

Even though Jack was excited about the progress he was making in the pursuit of his dream to be a recording star, the radio show didn't pay him anything for his efforts. In those days, radio performers needed a sponsor in order to be paid, and he didn't have one. Despite the lack of money, however, Jack considered this radio exposure to be an important learning experience and invaluable to his progress as a credible entertainer. Through this experience, he learned an important early lesson about the entertainment industry: sometimes, personal sacrifice is necessary for the greater cause.

While he was developing his radio show, Jack stayed in Fairview, but Marion left when she found a job doing housework elsewhere in Halifax. Even though he had been happy to be with his sister and hadn't minded helping her, Jack was relieved when she was able to earn an income and take care of herself. These were difficult times, and with no income he could hardly take care of himself; he would have been destitute if not for the generosity of the people who had opened their home to him.

Despite the lack of a steady income, Jack was pleased with the progress he was making in his career. Several months into his radio show, he told Landry he had been thinking about using a different name, and asked if he could be called "The Cowboy Blue Yodeler." The name was approved and Clarence Snow's early radio persona was born.

In the summer of 1934, Snow met Jack Faulkner, who also played guitar, and the two hit it off right away. They began practising their music together and quickly developed their own unique sound. It was Faulkner who actually suggested the duo take the show on the road, although touring towns and villages throughout Nova Scotia was not an easy feat in those days—especially considering neither had a vehicle. But when Jack's new friend pointed out that such a tour would allow The Cowboy Blue Yodeler to meet the fans who listened to him on CHNS, Jack immediately embraced Faulkner's concept; he understood that connecting with his fans would be important to his career, a philosophy he maintained throughout his life. To Jack, fans were always the number one priority.

In a borrowed car, with Faulkner as his companion, Jack Snow set out on the first tour of his professional music career. Billing themselves as: "The Cowboy Blue Yodeler and his side pal, Rambling Jack," the duo went into towns, rented small halls or schoolhouses,

Hank Snow in his early days, at CHNS in Halifax c.1940, wearing a shirt made by his mother.

put up their handmade posters, and then put on shows for the locals. Considering this was an era before modern sound equipment and staging, the shows were an overwhelming success: they played to packed houses and audiences with standing room only.

Their first venue was the Masonic Lodge Hall in Hubbards Cove, roughly fifty kilometres from Halifax. The facility held about fifty people and cost $2.50 to rent. Admission was $0.15 for children and $0.25 for adults, and on the night of the show they packed the place. From Hubbard's Cove, the duo took the show to Chester Basin, Lake Williams (near Bridgewater), and lastly to a small hall in Hunts Point, about eight kilometres from Liverpool, close enough for Jack's family and friends to catch the show. It was a thrill for Jack to perform in front of the hometown crowd and show them what he had achieved. It was a proud moment that he always treasured.

With the ten-day tour wrapped up following the Hunts Point show, the young musicians made their way back to Halifax, considering the effort a huge success. Of the tour, Jack often said it was what confirmed in his mind that he wanted to spend the rest of his life making music and entertaining audiences. He explained that while the modest tour had its problems, it had been a success in one important way: it had given him a small taste of show business, enough to make him want more.

Back in Halifax, Jack continued to do his Saturday night radio program for several months, until Landry started a weekly country music show called *Down on the Farm* and offered Jack a new opportunity. Landry asked Jack to perform each week, introducing him to a wider fan base. It was also at that time that Landry suggested Jack should change his name to "Hank," as it sounded more country. And just like that, "Hank Snow" was born. Since he was mostly singing country and western songs, Jack liked the new name, but he also added the title, "The Yodeling Ranger." He also changed the lyrics to his theme song.

He started his show with these lyrics:

> They call me the yodeling ranger,
> My badge is solid gold.
> I've rode the land by the Rio Grande
> And along that old ranger field.

And would finish with this verse:

> There's no place where I am a stranger,
> And I'm never lonely long,
> Wherever we are I have my old guitar
> And yodel this ranger song.

He would then wrap up with a yodel.

Snow would continue to be known as "Hank, The Yodeling Ranger" for several years, until he changed his name one last time, to "Hank, The Singing Ranger."

While continuing to struggle financially, it seemed like a great deal was starting to happen in Hank Snow's career. It was about this time that he met Minnie Blanche Aalders from Fairview. Hank wrote about the Halloween night they met at a social function in Fairview in his book: "I noticed a beautiful girl just as soon as I entered...I absolutely fell in love with Min that night."

Even though Minnie's parents weren't initially excited about the proposal and impending nuptials, since Hank was not gainfully employed and they questioned how he could provide for a wife, Hank and Minnie were married on September 2, 1935, in a simple ceremony at the English Church in Fairview. Despite any earlier objections raised by his new wife's parents, it was a happy occasion. Hank was married in a borrowed tuxedo with a new shirt that cost him $2.50, and a new $0.50 black bow tie. Minnie wore a new dress that she bought on credit.

Although their marriage got off to a rocky start because of Minnie's parents' dissension, Hank and Minnie's bond would last a lifetime. Their union survived difficult years of financial struggle, sometimes even destitution, as well as issues with Hank's drinking, extended separations while Hank pursued his dreams, and the demands that came with international stardom. Hank always said that he and Minnie were just meant to be together and that their love was strong enough to overcome any challenge that got in their way.

Hank often described this "special lady" as his inspiration and his strength. Referring to Minnie as his partner in life, he was also always quick to point out that she deserved a great deal of credit for his accomplishments throughout the years, as she often encouraged him to keep going or to take a risk when things got difficult. When Hank felt like giving up the music business and turning to something else to take care of his family, it was Minnie who pushed him on, saying that he had already gone too far to turn back.

But for the present, the newlyweds struggled. While the radio station may have been giving Hank the exposure he desired—and needed—to build an audience, it did not provide him with a regular paycheque. As he had done in the past when faced with a financial crunch, he took on various jobs—such as selling Fuller Brush products door to door—but, just like before, had little success as a salesman, and left the jobs as broke as when he started.

Hank and Minnie on their wedding day. The best man (far left) was Bill Reid, a local radio personality and steel guitar player, and the maid of honour (far right) was a friend of Minnie's named Margaret (last name unknown).

Frustrated with his inability in sales, Hank was desperate for work and was considering future options when representatives from the Texas-based Crazy Water Company called CHNS asking the station to produce a show that they could sponsor and that would promote their product, a laxative. They needed a small group of musicians, who the company would pay ten dollars a week, for the job. As part of the show, Hank was offered the chance to perform as a member of a combo that would feature a variety of musical styles. He was brought on to handle the country and western songs, which suited

Hank Snow and his gang as they played on CHNS.

him perfectly fine. *The Crazy Water Crystals Show* went on the air at noon every day except Saturday, for fifteen minutes. Now Hank had a real paying job on the radio.

More good luck came Hank's way when the CBC asked him to do some programs on the Maritime Broadcasting Network for a show called *Farm Hour.* He would receive twenty-six dollars each time he did the show, about once every two months, but it wasn't as much about the money for Hank as it was about expanding his audience.

With the increased exposure came more opportunities for Hank to pursue his dream of becoming a full-fledged entertainer, such as getting a call to play the Gaiety Theatre in downtown Halifax. He earned twelve dollars for a three-day run doing a twenty-minute show before the movie matinee and another before the evening movie. Hank saw this as yet another chance to increase his exposure, especially since this live audience was about three hundred, his largest up to that date.

To help him look his best, Hank's mother made him a white satin shirt with full sleeves, a wide collar with a red star sewn on each tip, and a big red star on each breast. The collar also had a black border and black silk laces that went up the front. To complete the look, Hank bought a pair of black dungarees for $2.75 and Minnie sewed a narrow white cotton stripe down the side of each leg. She also made him a neckerchief out of orange and red cloth, which he cherished and wore with pride for years. Dressed to impress, it was on that day Hank promised himself that whenever he appeared on stage, he would wear the most decorative suits he could find; thus was born the trademark style for which Hank Snow eventually became famous.

Things were finally starting to happen for Hank, but there was more to come. Following one of his shows at CHNS, Landry suggested that he should consider writing a letter to RCA Victor in Montreal to see if he could get an audition and maybe get added to their roster of artists. Landry thought Hank was good enough to make records and encouraged him to take a chance. Hank thought it was a long shot at best, but a shot nonetheless.

With Landry's prodding, on April 9, 1935, Hank wrote a letter to A. H. Joseph, manager of the Repertoire and Recording Department for RCA Victor in Montreal. On April 18, Hank received a response, basically a rejection letter. But, like before, he chose to see the response as positive and would not accept "no" for an answer.

It may have been his earlier struggles with poverty that gave him his drive, determination, and fighting spirit, but rejection was not an option for Hank. He filed the letter away but knew he would be going to Montreal sometime in the future, though he didn't yet know when or how.

THE MUSIC MAN

For Love and Music

Following their wedding, Hank and Minnie bought second-hand furniture and moved into their first apartment. Located on Barrington Street in downtown Halifax, the place was small, consisting of one bedroom and a kitchen. They shared a bathroom with the building's other tenants. The compact, dingy rooms weren't much to brag about, but with Minnie's personal touches and a good cleaning, the newlyweds made it their home and were happy there. Within a short time, Minnie became pregnant, and by early the next year the couple had moved into a more centrally located apartment. It was as tiny as the first place, and with a baby on the way the couple quickly realized it wouldn't be sufficient for the needs of a growing family. They immediately relocated to a larger place, but it was so filthy that they moved out within a day, and into another two-room apartment on Artz Street, between Barrington and Brunswick Streets. It wasn't much, Hank would always say about the small apartment, but it was their home. Compared to some of the places Hank had lived throughout his life, this place wasn't so bad, and being with Minnie was all that mattered to him.

Around this time, the musical director of CHNS, Dick Frye, gave Hank some sheet music samples and suggested he should learn to read it; he thought the talented young singer and guitar player could benefit from such knowledge. Although Hank had never before tried to read music, this actually sounded liked a good idea to him, and so he began taking music lessons for fifty cents a week. He would

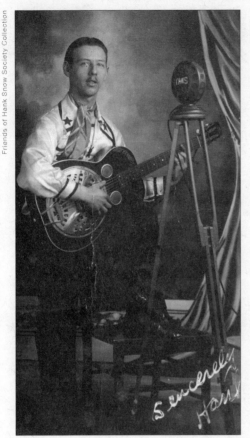
Friends of Hank Snow Society Collection

This undated photo shows Hank Snow in his early days on CHNS.

later say they were among the best investments he had ever made, and he remained grateful that Frye had made the suggestion.

Within a short time, spurred on by his newly acquired musical knowledge, Hank began thinking of going to Montreal, but not before welcoming his new baby. On February 6, 1936, following a difficult delivery for Minnie, the couple welcomed their son, Jimmie Rodgers Snow (named after Hank's idol). Jimmie was born in the charity ward at the Salvation Army hospital in Halifax, and due to complications during delivery, doctors warned Minnie that she should not have any more children—not the kind of news a young married couple wants to hear. But Hank and Minnie took the advice to heart, and Jimmie was to be their only child. The care that the new parents received at the hospital led to Hank's lifelong appreciation of the Salvation Army, an organization he supported throughout the years whenever possible. (In fact, Hank so appreciated their work that following his death in 1999, he bequeathed one hundred thousand dollars to the Salvation Army in his will.)

With Minnie now at home taking care of the baby, she was unable to continue her job at the Moirs chocolate factory, for which she had been earning six dollars a week. This reality put more pressure on Hank. Without Minnie's income, the family was forced to live on the ten dollars a week Hank was earning from *The Crazy Water Crystals Show* at CHNS. But no matter how difficult it became for them to make ends meet, Hank never gave up his dream of someday recording with RCA Victor, and he planned to make his way to Montreal just as soon as financially possible.

While biding his time, Hank continued to practise and perfect his vocal and musical skills, learning as much about music as he could absorb. Shortly after Jimmie's birth, he wrote his first song, "The Night I Stole Ole Sammy Morgan's Gin." (In all, throughout his legendary career, Hank estimated he composed about one hundred and fifty songs, though some musical historians credit him with many more than that, claiming he wrote hundreds. It's difficult to pinpoint the exact number, as it's likely some were lost or destroyed.)

Despite the difficult financial times they faced, Hank and Minnie somehow managed to scrape by on Hank's meagre wages, which were supplemented by the extra five dollars he occasionally earned doing shows at various Halifax theatres, including the Community Theatre on Gottingen Street as well as the Family Theatre and newly opened Capitol Theatre on Barrington Street. But as sometimes happens in life, the situation soon took a turn for the worse. When Crazy Water Crystals pulled its sponsorship and the program went off the air, Hank was left scrambling for money. As the program had been his only means of steady income, Hank was sick with fear and anxiety. Forget about any future plans for Montreal, first and foremost on his mind were the well-being of his wife and baby.

With no food, no milk for Jimmie, and no money to pay the bills, the Snows were destitute, and Hank felt like a failure for being unable to provide for his loved ones. Finally, with no other means to support his family, Hank was forced to do something he hated to do: he had to accept pay from the city. For working one full day on the city streets, Hank was given $2.50 worth of food tickets each week along with tickets for a small paper bag of coal, used to fire up the stove in their apartment. This was Hank and Minnie's only source of heating and their only means of cooking. Workers also received a quart of milk daily for their efforts. This was still the height of the Depression, and Hank knew this money was necessary for his family's survival, so he put his personal pride aside.

Hank didn't have to like the situation, and he would never call it "welfare," because he had to work in order to receive, but he felt he had no other choice. Hank often said those tickets were heaven sent, but he also admitted that it was not easy to accept what many people viewed as charity. Never one to easily accept handouts, Hank believed in making his own way. But sometimes reality dictates one's circumstances, and so it was that Hank reluctantly lined up with the hundreds of others in the same predicament, and received his assignment. He was sent to work in front of the Lord Nelson Hotel, where CHNS was located. There, he was required to pick ice off the street with a shovel and load it onto city trucks. Embarrassed at the thought that some of his former colleagues from the station might see him there, Hank only stayed one day on the job. Following that, he told Minnie they would have to find other ways to make ends meet; he could not face that shame ever again.

Once Minnie had recovered from her difficult delivery and was back on her feet, she left Jimmie in the care of a sitter and went back to work at the chocolate factory to help out with the bills. By this time Hank felt he was good enough at reading music to give guitar lessons. He charged fifty cents per session. But it was around this time that the family was forced to leave their Artz Street apartment: they had fallen behind in their rent. A friend in Dartmouth partitioned his garage into three rooms and allowed the family to stay there. It wasn't much, but with a little tender loving care from Minnie the place became their home, and Hank later said it wasn't as bad as it might seem. It was warm and dry, and considering their predicament, they had few alternatives.

Just when things were starting to look bleak, a promoter, Bert Anstice, heard Hank's show on the Maritime Network and asked if he would be interested in touring as part of a new travelling western swing band. Hank was asked to play guitar and sing western songs, for which he would earn fifteen dollars a week plus food and lodging on the road. The band played at venues throughout the Maritimes every Monday through Saturday. Hank immediately jumped at the offer.

Through this experience, Hank was introduced to the concept of band members wearing uniforms when they played. While Hank wore his own clothing on stage, as he was not a member of the band,

Anstice supplied outfits to the others. These uniforms consisted of gray flannel pants, a dark blue jacket with gold-braid trim and the gold-braided letters "M. B." on the breast pocket, as the band was known as Bert Anstice and the Mountain Boys.

Bert had arranged with the CBC that the band would play each Saturday night show wherever there was an affiliate station—which could have been Halifax, Charlottetown, Sydney, or Saint John—and the set would be broadcast across Canada. Hank worked for Anstice for three months, time that he always considered to be an important part in the advancement of his career, largely because of the experience he received on the road. However, the relationship between the two men ended badly when, after deducting all his expenses, Anstice could not pay his band members for their time. Hank never did get the full wages he was owed.

Shortly after the tour ended, the Snow family moved from Dartmouth and relocated to a small two-bedroom apartment on Agricola Street. Still pressed for money, Hank was given the chance to participate in another show on CHNS radio—but with no sponsorship and therefore no pay. The family continued to struggle financially.

In October 1936, faced with a growing financial crisis, fed up with living in poverty, and having a wife and baby to care for, Hank decided that if he was ever going to go to Montreal, it was now or never. If it was going to be never, then he had to accept the reality and do something else to support his family, because they could not continue living in such poor conditions. If music wasn't going to fulfill his dreams then he had to change course, but he felt compelled to take the next step. Despite the earlier letter from A. H. Joseph, Hank was determined to secure a recording contract with RCA Victor, and he would not be deterred.

Off to Montreal

So it was that in October 1936, Hank wrote to A. H. Joseph at RCA Victor telling him when he would be in Montreal. Joseph quickly replied, informing Hank that he would arrange for a meeting and an audition upon his arrival. Hank was excited at the prospect of finally getting into a recording studio and maybe even landing a contract. Everything was set, except for the cost of getting there. However, spurred on by Joseph's response and with Minnie's blessing, Hank managed to scrape together sufficient funds to make the trip.

Using the few cents he had earned from the guitar lessons he gave every week, Hank was able to buy a round-trip coach ticket on one of the passenger trains leaving Halifax daily for Montreal. He was on his way with thirteen dollars in his pocket, his old beat-up suitcase, held together with rope, and the Regal Zonophone guitar that he'd bought with the money he'd earned from the Bert Anstice tour.

The trip took two days. When Hank got to Montreal, he immediately found a cheap hotel room that was just big enough for a cot and a chair and hardly large enough for him, his suitcase, and guitar. He often joked it was more like a closet than a hotel room, but he was so excited to be there that it didn't really matter where he slept.

The next morning Hank called Joseph, who agreed to meet him at two o'clock that same afternoon. Hank had no idea what to expect from the session, but he was thrilled to finally meet the man responsible for signing new artists to RCA Victor. The meeting went well, as they talked about Hank's favourite music and artists that had influenced his style, but Joseph threw Hank for a loop when he told him the label would only be interested in him if he had original songs to record. On the spur of the moment—and overwhelmed with the excitement of finally being in Montreal—Hank quickly told the record company executive that he had, indeed, written several songs that he'd be performing for his audition. He hadn't.

The audition was set for the next day at 2:00 P.M. This was the opportunity that Hank had been working toward for years, and he couldn't believe it was finally happening. Now all he had to do was write some original songs before the next afternoon—a daunting prospect, as Hank had never considered himself to be a songwriter. However, he reasoned, that would have to change quickly if he was going to make this work. He had come too far to blow this opportunity without giving it everything he had.

That night, back in his tiny hotel room, Hank quickly wrote two songs: one called "Lonesome Blue Yodel" written in the Jimmie Rodgers style and based on a series of Rodgers's songs by the same title, and the other he called "The Prisoned Cowboy. Everything Hank had ever dreamed of and worked for was riding on this audition. He knew he had one opportunity to impress Joseph. If not, he'd have to go back to Halifax and do something else with his life. He wasn't prepared to do that.

Two hours early, at noon on October 29, 1936, with his guitar over his back and his two songs in his back pocket, Hank Snow walked into the recording studio, which was actually an old church, as the RCA studios were undergoing renovations at that time, and prepared to meet his destiny. There he met Joseph and the company's recording engineer, and the session was underway. Hank made his first recording, "The Prisoned Cowboy," in two takes. Then he recorded "Lonesome Blue Yodel," and just like that, the first recording session of Hank Snow's career was over. When Hank left that day, he had no idea what would happen next, but Joseph told him to go back home to Nova Scotia to be with his family. He assured Hank he would be in touch once the company determined if the records were good enough to release.

With all his hopes for the future resting on those two records, Hank boarded the train and headed back to Halifax to await word from RCA Victor. While he really didn't know what to think about how things had gone, he was sure he had done his best. If nothing else, he could take some comfort in the fact that he had at least rolled the dice and taken the chance—something many people never have the courage to do. It may have been small consolation, but if it didn't work out, at least Hank could say he'd tried.

As could be expected, the waiting was difficult, especially with so much riding on the audition. Back in Halifax, Hank bided his time, earning a few dollars wherever he could, teaching guitar and doing the occasional small job. Weeks went by without a word, and just when Hank was ready to accept defeat, a letter arrived from Montreal. Joseph told him they had listened to his recordings and were so impressed with what he had done that they decided to release his songs on the RCA Victor Bluebird label. Hank later said that when he had first heard the records, he hated how they sounded so tinny and hollow, but Joseph had clearly heard something in the recordings that Hank couldn't, because he also sent along the first royalty cheque of Hank's career, in the amount of $1.96.

The man Hank credited for starting Hank Snow off on his long career, A. H. Joseph (right). Joseph recorded Hank's voice for the first time at RCA Victor in Montreal, on October 29, 1936.

Times were still tough for the Snows, and Hank knew that if he was going to make it in the entertainment business he had to be aggressive and pursue opportunities. Inspired by his real-life hardships, Hank's songwriting abilities blossomed. By late 1937, armed with an inventory of new songs, Hank wrote to Joseph asking if he would record him again. Joseph was so impressed by the results of the first session that he quickly confirmed new recording dates. This time, though, still disappointed with the sound of the first recordings, Hank planned to use a steel guitar player to improve the quality of his sound.

Again with the meagre funds he managed to scrape together, he bought a train ticket to Montreal, where he stayed in the same cheap hotel room as the year before. Using contacts he'd made through a music store in the city, he tracked down a well-regarded steel guitar player named Eugene "Johnny" Beaudoin. They hit it off right away, forming a quick bond that lasted a lifetime.

During the four-day session, from November 6 to 9, 1937, Hank, backed by his steel guitar player, recorded eight songs for RCA Victor. After that, he went back to Halifax and waited. Two months later, he received the records and word from Joseph. Hank had no idea that one of these original songs, "The Blue Velvet Band," was destined to become a smash hit—his first—in Canada. However, before he discovered what it was like to have a hit record, Hank had to face a sudden health threat.

Shortly after Hank's return from Montreal, the Snows moved again, this time to a small house on Lawrence Street. Hank was soon diagnosed with wet pleurisy and had to be under a doctor's care for more than a year. Nevertheless, despite his ill health, things eventually began to get a little easier for the family in their new location. Through Hank's guitar lessons, the arrival of the occasional royalty cheque from RCA Victor, and with a few lucky breaks, the family managed to find the money to have their own telephone installed—a big deal in those days—and Hank bought a new guitar: a D-28 Martin. He even managed to save enough money to buy a car: a dark blue Chevrolet coupe, for which he paid three hundred dollars. The situation improved even more when CHNS offered Hank a job hosting the station's new weekday morning show. He would receive ten dollars a week for the effort, which was a good pay for him, and the show also gave him the opportunity to try out new songs as he wrote them before taking them to Montreal for future recording sessions. All was good for Hank at this point in his life, for now at least.

Hank was almost fully recuperated and feeling much improved when the famous Barnum & Bailey Circus, featuring star Hoot Gibson, one of the biggest silent-Western actors at the time, came to Halifax. Hank had to see him. As he watched, he found himself becoming enamoured with the trick-riding stunts Gibson and the other cowboys performed on their horses. It was the first time Hank had ever seen such a spectacle, and from that point on he was inspired to follow their example.

As 1939 came to an end and RCA Victor was steadily releasing Hank's records, he began searching for talented musicians to play with him on the road. He spent several months calling on musicians he had previously met, and after auditioning a handful he managed to put together a lineup he felt comfortable playing with. With his band and a good car to get them around—a 1934 Ford he purchased after getting rid of the Chevrolet—Hank was ready to take his show on the road, keeping his appearances to within a 250-kilometre radius of Halifax. The first show he booked was at Lantz Siding, a tiny hall owned by the Odd Fellows that held roughly three hundred chairs. It cost three dollars to rent for one Saturday night, but it was worth the fee. The show was standing room only with a lineup of people waiting outside. Hank was impressed that so many good people would turn out to see him perform, and after covering his expenses, he managed a profit of thirty dollars. All in a good night's work, he figured, and it put some extra money in his pocket, which he could reinvest in future shows.

That night, Hank felt he was finally being accepted as a professional entertainer. All his hard work and sacrifice was finally starting to pay off. Still, he had a lot to learn about the music business: promotion, road expenses, paying the wages for his backup musicians and all necessary government taxes and professional fees. There were many facets of the industry that Hank had not considered, but over the next few months he studied the business and taught himself everything he needed to know about booking, touring, and promoting. A great deal of it was trial and error, but Hank learned the ropes from those early experiences and, in time, he was managing his operation like a seasoned pro.

Eventually, Hank took his show, which was growing with the addition of new entertainers and musicians, throughout Nova Scotia, playing in various concert halls and school auditoriums. The more he played, the more his popularity and name recognition grew. He may not have been getting rich, but to him, these performances were valuable training experiences from which he could springboard into bigger and better things. Around this time, CHNS told Hank that another sponsor, Lambert Cough Medicine Company, had expressed interest in using him for a new thirty-minute show they were proposing for the station, and to his pleasure, Hank could use the same musicians that played with him on the road, something that was important to him. The company would also pay Hank and his band for their efforts, which, of course, was music to Hank's ears.

As the months went by and Hank and his band continued to improve the quality of their sound, he decided it was time to spruce up their appearance; he felt image was important. Recalling his earlier experiences on the Bert Anstice tour, Hank ordered every band member a western shirt and a neckerchief from a large western store located in Denver, Colorado, that he had seen advertised in a magazine, and had them shipped to Halifax. He also got the members each a straw hat, which he painted black, and around which he added a narrow white strip of cloth. With his band sharply outfitted, Hank chose to wear a regular western hat and the white satin shirt that his mother had made for him, the one with the red felt stars on the breast and both collars. Together, they made an impressive-looking group.

Hank and his gang were soon travelling the roads of Nova Scotia, many of which were nothing more than narrow wagon paths, still unpaved and nearly impassible, especially during the inclement weather that always seemed to hit when they had a show outside the city limits. Jammed into Hank's Ford, pulling a small, two-wheeled trailer they had picked up for next to nothing to haul their equipment and instruments, they hit the road like early troubadours, venturing beyond their Halifax base of operations and expanding their territory, all the while attracting a larger audience.

With his regular radio shows, steady clientele of guitar students, and weekend appearances continuing to provide a steady income, things were looking up for Hank. With finances improving, the Snow family moved again, this time into an apartment over a grocery store on Oxford Street. It was the best place Hank and Minnie had lived in up to that point. No longer feeling the pinch of poverty, Hank could now concentrate all of his creative juices on his quickly growing musical career. It was a good feeling.

The Hits Keep Coming

On the strength of the eight songs Hank Snow had recorded in Montreal in 1937, which were gradually released by RCA Victor, his reputation as The Yodeling Ranger spread across the country. In 1939 Hank returned to Montreal and recorded six more songs on the Bluebird label, thus assuring him steady progress in the entertainment world, but his fame wasn't the only thing growing. Royalty cheques were rolling in four times a year, ranging anywhere from $85 to $150, a great deal of money in those days—enough to convince

Hank's gang from 1940.

him that he was finally on the road to making it big. If he'd had doubts before, these regular cheques erased them and gave Hank the incentive to push harder.

Things were going so well for Hank that Minnie quit her job at the Moirs factory to stay at home and take care of Jimmie, who was just shy of five. Hank really felt that the Snows were on their way at long last, which meant another move was imminent. They found a small but comfortable home on Dutch Village Road, close to Minnie's parents' place.

In keeping with his new-found status as a rising country music star, Hank got rid of his 1934 Ford and bought a 1938 Plymouth for sixty dollars a month. As demand for his personal appearances picked up and his travels throughout the Maritimes increased, he thought it would be prudent to buy a house trailer where he and his band could stay after their shows instead of driving home each night, a good distance in some cases. He bought a six-metre trailer in Lunenburg for $150, allowing Hank and the band to stay on the road for several days at a time and reduce travel costs.

Their trailer gave the band great freedom. After cleaning it up and adding a few amenities, such as mattresses and window curtains, and painting "Hank Snow, The Yodeling Ranger" on the outside, the band hit the road, and often the family would also come along. In Hank's mind, this was the ultimate test of his still fledgling career: could he make enough money through his music to pay the bills and his musicians, and still have enough left over to support himself and his family? It was a gamble, but it was one he had to take.

With their routes through Nova Scotia, Cape Breton, New Brunswick, and Prince Edward Island carefully mapped, Hank and his group hit the road, playing at dance halls and school gymnasiums in front of large audiences. The rent for these places was usually between two to three dollars a night—a considerable price in the 1930s—but by this time, Hank had to play venues that could hold several hundred people; there was no other option.

As the show drew larger audiences, Hank also began to understand the value of investing in his career. He realized that in order to truly succeed, he would have to spend money, so he invested in better-quality sound equipment, paid for professionally printed posters and advertising, and bought new uniforms for his band. The one- to three-week tours were a huge success, generating a profit between $75 and $150 a night.

With wider exposure came increased demand from fans, and as Hank Snow's reputation grew so did the touring schedule. For much of the early 1940s, Hank and his band travelled extensively throughout the Maritimes and even began expanding into eastern Quebec. By the fall of 1941, buoyed by his growing success and increased popularity, Hank decided that he was ready to leave Halifax and move to Montreal to be closer to RCA Victor and, he hoped, to find a bigger audience.

Despite opposition from family and friends, who insisted he was foolish to give up everything he had worked so hard to establish in Halifax, Hank was ready to test a larger market. While he agreed that Halifax and the rest of the Maritimes had been good to him, an unknown singer from Brooklyn, Queens County, with a guitar, he had loftier goals and bigger dreams. He understood that it would be difficult to leave everything behind, but he wanted to be a big country music star like those he had grown up listening to on the radio, and he felt the only way to achieve that level of success was to move to a place that had a broader reach. In fact, Hank saw Montreal as just a stop along the way. He planned on eventually going to the United States, where there was an even bigger market for his music. Ultimately, he wanted to play on the American radio stations he had been tuning into for years, such as WWVA in Wheeling, West Virginia, but to do that he knew he had to be prepared to leave Nova Scotia. That time had come.

Moving to Montreal meant Hank had to give up the steady income from his concerts and other appearances, but Minnie agreed that if he was ever going to make it big, it was the right move. With her blessing, their personal belongings in storage, and their 1938 Plymouth sold, Hank and his family took the train to Montreal. Once there, they briefly stayed with Johnny Beaudoin, the steel guitar player on Hank's earlier recordings, and his family. Though the Snows were welcome to stay as long as they liked, the family eventually found a cheap one-room apartment in east Montreal.

Hank always said he found the city to be a disappointment; nothing seemed to click for him there. Although he went job-hunting, he couldn't find work, and the fact that most people could only communicate in French made it extremely difficult for him and his family. Financially they were on a tight budget, which only added to the stress and frustration. Hank feared he had made a huge mistake leaving Halifax.

During his time in Montreal, Hank managed to land only one job, as the opening act for some performer he had never heard of. Because the audience was mostly made up of francophones who could not understand his lyrics, Hank ultimately considered the show a failure. It certainly wasn't the kind of reception to which he had grown accustomed in Nova Scotia.

By December 7, 1941, when word came that the Japanese had attacked Pearl Harbour and the U.S. was now at war, the Snows were running short on money and Hank was running low on patience. Weighing his options, Hank was ready to call it a day in Montreal and move back to Halifax, where he hoped he could rebuild some of the success he had given up. But just then an opportunity presented itself. Hank received a letter from Stan Chapman in Campbellton, New Brunswick, who was responding to an earlier letter Hank had sent asking about work. Since the station was already playing Hank's Bluebird records, they were familiar with The Yodeling Ranger, and Chapman offered him a job at CKNB Campbellton, a one thousand-watt station.

Jumping at the opportunity to leave Montreal and excited at the prospect of working in radio again, Hank, along with Minnie and Jimmie, left the city by train in February 1942. It was about a day's ride to Campbellton, where Hank disembarked alone. Minnie and Jimmie continued to Halifax, where they would stay with her parents until Hank had enough money to provide them a home. He would send for them when he was re-established.

Hank was immediately welcomed at his new location. Chapman and his wife made him feel right at home, while the station's two announcers, Jimmy Wood and Dick Dickerson, helped him get established in his new surroundings. Chapman was the first to suggest that Hank make extra money by printing a book of his songs and selling it over the radio. Hank thought this was a great idea and he did just that, selling *The Hank Snow Songbook* along with a photograph of himself with his former band from Halifax and a list of his RCA Bluebird recordings. Copies went for fifteen cents apiece. Hank often recalled that he sold lots of those books, as it seemed his songs were pretty popular with other singers and guitar players.

Along with his radio work in Campbellton, Hank also began making personal appearances again. He was surprised at how good it felt to be up on stage in front of a live audience again. It was where he was meant to be. And by year's end, he hoped Minnie and Jimmie would return to be with him. For now, though, it was down to business. With this return to the atmosphere in which he felt comfortable, Hank was soon back in the groove, picking up where he'd left off in Halifax. His disappointing side venture to Montreal soon became nothing more than a bad memory—a footnote in his climb up the entertainment ladder. Within a short time, Hank had managed to put the experience behind him and move on. Dwelling on past failures was not his style.

As Hank's radio program expanded and grew in popularity, Chapman introduced him to Gordon Gaisley, manager of the Campbellton's Capitol Theatre. In turn, Gaisley offered Hank a steady weekend job playing between the Friday and Saturday movies. Hank earned twenty-five dollars for a two-day run every week, thirty-five if he added a third day. Not only was the money good,

Hank Snow, The Yodeling Ranger, from his CKCW days in Moncton.

but the Campbellton location was part of chain of a dozen theatres throughout New Brunswick, Nova Scotia, and Prince Edward Island, owned by F. G. Spencer. Hank knew that if things went well, this opportunity could open a lot of possibilities for him.

By the fall of 1942, Hank had contacted Fred Lynds, manager of CKCW in Moncton, asking about possible work. Based on his growing reputation through CKNB, his RCA records, and his personal appearances, Lynds offered Hank a program on the station. Once established in Moncton, Hank planned to move his family there with him.

At CKCW, Hank would earn twenty-five dollars for one show a week, which would be increased if shows were sponsored. Although it was good deal, Hank put the offer on hold: around the same time, Spencer gave him the opportunity to tour his entire theatre circuit. Thinking it was a good chance to expand his presence, Hank jumped at the opportunity to perform. From those appearances, he was offered tours at other theatre chains, and within months he was moving throughout the Maritimes on a regular circuit, all the while watching his audience grow.

Not only was Hank Snow now a well-known radio personality and recording artist, but by the end of 1942 he had also established himself as a major live attraction in the Maritimes.

The Singing Ranger

Once the tour wrapped up, Hank went back to CKCW in Moncton, where Lynds gave him a half-hour show at seven o'clock every night, Monday through Saturday. By this time Hank had become pretty well established in New Brunswick, and continued to make personal appearances in the nearby towns and villages. No matter how much success Hank achieved as a recording artist, he believed the most important part of the business was the live performance, as these shows gave him the opportunity to connect with the audience and to see, first-hand, their reaction to his music. He thrived on that feedback, soaking it up and learning from it, all with the goal of becoming an even better performer.

In April 1943, the Capitol Theatre managers asked Hank to do their circuit again, but in order for him to continue touring and keep his job in Moncton, he needed a car. He found a 1941 Buick Roadmaster for $2,200. This was a great deal of money, but Hank wanted the car the minute he saw it and he knew he just had to have it. Not only would the car solve his transportation issues, but it also fit his image; it was the kind of vehicle a successful entertainer should be driving. Impressions were important to Hank even at that stage of his career, and although it was risky, he arranged a bank loan and bought the Buick. He was now touring in comfort throughout the province and basking in the limelight.

Meanwhile, as Hank was busy building his career in the Maritimes, his RCA Victor records were still in high rotation throughout Canada. He soon received word that another of his hastily written songs, "Wandering On," had become a hit across the country, just as "The Blue Velvet Band" had done a year earlier. Because Hank had recorded so many songs for RCA Victor during those earlier trips to Montreal, the record company had a steady stream of new material to release at certain intervals, a move designed to propel his career to new heights. But in 1942, amid a contractual dispute between the major record labels and the American Federation of Musicians union, his momentum was nearly derailed as the labour action almost halted his next trip to Montreal. With his career kicking into high gear, Hank was devastated at the prospect of losing any ground he had

Hank Snow being recorded by CBC radio in 1942.

established. He knew that any delay could set him back by months; he had worked too hard to stand by and watch that happen, but the situation was out of his hands.

Notwithstanding the drawn-out contract dispute, in May 1943, Joseph at RCA Victor arranged a secret recording session for Hank and his musicians, during which they recorded sixteen songs for future release. Among those recordings were what are now considered Hank Snow classics: "We'll Never Say Goodbye, Just So Long," "When My Blue Moon Turns to Gold Again," "Heartsick and Lonely," "Rose of the Rio," and "Goodnight, Little Buckaroo."

Over the next few months, Hank continued to use Moncton as his home base while hosting his radio show and touring throughout the Maritimes in his 1941 Buick Roadmaster. By 1944, and unbeknownst to him, Hank's success as a Canadian country music singer had somehow spread south of the border. Early that year he received a letter postmarked Browder, Kentucky, from a woman named Willidean Stephenson. He had no idea who she was, but she explained to him that she had heard Hank's music on a Canadian radio station and she liked it.

This letter, his first from an American fan, excited and inspired Hank. But Stephenson was more than just a fan. In fact, she became the catalyst that would lead Hank to the United States. As it turns out, Stephenson had told a promoter named Jack Howard from Philadelphia, Pennsylvania, about Hank Snow, The Yodeling Ranger, who was making a name for himself in Canada. Howard, who also ran a music publishing company, was so impressed that, following some correspondence, he invited Hank to spend time with him in Philadelphia. Howard was confident, based on what he had heard, that he could arrange for Hank to appear on some American shows, a move that would introduce him to a whole new market. This was the perfect opportunity for Hank, as he had also been corresponding with Big Slim McAuliffe, The Lone Cowboy, for about a year prior to Howard's invitation. Big Slim was a popular singer on the *Wheeling Jamboree* that was broadcast on WWVA, a fifty thousand-watt station originating from Wheeling, West Virginia, that could reach the Maritimes. Hank often listened to the show. Slim had invited Hank to visit him in Wheeling and Hank asked Jack Howard to go with him, thus establishing a relationship that Hank would treasure his entire life.

Hank Snow was finally on the verge of the United States breakthrough he had long dreamed of, but the world was still in the throes of the Second World War and Canada had recently implemented the draft, so his rise to international fame would not be without its obstacles. When Hank received a letter in February from the Canadian Army telling him to report for a physical examination in Fredericton, New Brunswick, his dreams were nearly shattered by the prospect of being sent overseas. He feared his plans were in danger of stalling, but he was prepared to do his part for the cause if he was called upon to do so.

As ordered, Hank turned up in Fredericton on March 15, 1944, and was prepared for the worst. However, when his physical exam revealed a deformity in one of his lungs, which doctors blamed on the

Hank and Big Slim.

earlier pleurisy he had suffered with for over a year, he was rejected, deemed unqualified for active duty due to medical reasons. The path was now cleared for Hank to pursue his professional recording career, and he seized the moment.

While making plans to travel to the U.S., Hank continued to tour the Maritime theatre circuit, all the while striving to expand his celebrity status. He knew, even then, how important it was to continue reaching new audiences. It was during one of those stops in the summer of 1944 at a show in Amherst, Nova Scotia, that the theatre manager asked Hank why he used the name "The Yodeling Ranger" when, in fact, he never yodelled during his performance. The truth was, early in his career, Hank had yodelled, but he'd given it up after his voice had changed and it became difficult for him to hit certain notes. Hank thought about the question and decided the theatre manager raised a valid point. From that point on, Hank Snow billed himself as "The Singing Ranger," and the name stuck for the rest of his life.

During this time, Hank maintained close contact with Big Slim, who continued to persuade him to come to Wheeling. With job enticements and promises of work, Hank was anxious to go to the U.S., where he believed his big break awaited him. The final inducement was the suggestion that Big Slim would talk to the manager of station

WWVA about letting Hank perform on the *Wheeling Jamboree*, a suggestion that was very appealing to him. Hank was also taken with the idea of learning trick riding and roping from Big Slim, who was known as a real cowboy, and was anxious to finally meet the man with whom he had been corresponding for some time.

In the middle of July 1944, Hank boarded a train in Moncton and made his way south of the border to Philadelphia, where he met Jack Howard for the first time. The two men became immediate friends and Hank often referred to Howard as a "fine person," a "great promoter," and a man who played a vital role in helping him become established in the American market. Prior to Hank's arrival, Howard had arranged several promotional appearances for Hank. His first show ever in the United States was at a well-known venue in downtown Philadelphia called the Labor Plaza, where he performed for an estimated five thousand servicemen, his largest live audience up to that point. Hank did many radio interviews over the next couple of days, and was thrilled to be well received by appreciative American audiences.

After the promotional blitz in Philadelphia, Hank and Howard took the train to Wheeling, West Virginia, where, for the first time, they met with Big Slim at WWVA located on the top floor of the Hawley Building in the city's downtown area. Hank was impressed with the tall, slender cowboy right away. The pair hit it off immediately, and following the meeting, Slim invited Hank and Howard to his home and stables. It was there that Hank had his introduction to horses and trick riding, a skill he would soon learn and perfect, and eventually incorporate into his act.

During that trip, Slim, a well-known entertainer, suggested to Hank that he permanently relocate to West Virginia, where, with his support and contacts, he felt that Hank could successfully pursue his music career. Hank liked the idea and became determined to do just that. Almost immediately, he began formulating plans for the move, providing Minnie was on board with the idea. She had always stood behind him in the past, no matter the risk or the obstacles he threw at her, and he believed she would agree that this would be a good career move for him.

Upon their return to Philadelphia, Howard took Hank to the famous Globe Western Tailors, where Hank met the acclaimed tailor

Promotional photograph of Hank Snow taken in Philadelphia.

Rodeo Ben and was fitted for his first-ever suit, custom-made to his specifications: powder blue with gold trim. Stage appearance was already very important to Hank, and these "flashy" outfits would soon become synonymous with the name "Hank Snow."

Following this trip, Hank became consumed with the idea of moving to the United States. Slim's offer appealed to him for many reasons, including the friendship that he had just begun with Jack Howard. Hank dreamed of having his music accepted by the larger American audience and of "making it big" in that lucrative market where country music was already becoming more popular. By the time he arrived back in Moncton, Hank had decided that he and his

An early Hank Snow showing off his riding skills. Possibly taken at the Cumberland County Fair. Date unknown.

family would move to Wheeling, where he felt he could take the next step on the road to his musical career. To his relief, Minnie said he should do it, and with her support and encouragement, he set about making it happen.

SOUTH OF THE BORDER

The Wheeling Jamboree

Following his trip to the U.S., Hank concentrated much of his efforts on relocating to West Virginia. Back in New Brunswick, he hit the ground running, doing the theatre circuit and resuming his radio show on CKCW, always with an eye to taking the next step in his career. On December 20, 1944, motivated by his future plans, Hank travelled to Montreal for another recording session at RCA Victor. Over a four-day period, he recorded eighteen new songs, many of which went on to become Hank Snow classics: "Your Little Band of Gold," "Soldier's Last Letter," "Blue Ranger," "You Broke the Chain That Held Our Hearts," and "You Played Love on the Strings of My Heart," which went on to become one of Hank's biggest hits in Canada.

Hank's decision to move to the United States had nothing to do with any discontent he may have felt about his success in Canada. In fact, in a 1991 interview with this author, he insisted that just the opposite was true and that, in fact, he owed a great deal to his native country; he felt he owed Canadians a debt that he could never repay. "The Canadian people have always been extremely supportive of me," he said while speaking from his Nashville office. But, as he pointed out, it was necessary to follow the business opportunities wherever they took him, so it was with that drive and determination that the family moved south of the border.

> It was a struggle at first, and I went to the United
> States because that's where the opportunities were. But

despite whatever success I had in the United States, the people in Canada always remained very important to me. In those days when I was starting out, there wasn't much of a country music business in Canada so you had to look to other places. There were many people in Canada who helped me along the way [and] I'm grateful to them.

Following that stopover in Montreal, Hank and Minnie loaded eight-year-old Jimmie and all their personal belongings into the Buick and headed to Wheeling, unaware of—and unprepared for—what the future held for them. Hank, however, went with the hope that he would make his big break there. The Snows spent the Christmas of 1944 in West Virginia with Slim and his wife, Hazel. Immediately after the holidays the Snows got a room in town at the Wheeling Hotel, where many of the *Jamboree* performers stayed when they were in town.

In keeping to his word, Slim arranged a meeting between Hank and George W. Smith, the station manager at WWVA. Hank was required to audition by reading several commercials in the studio. He was a natural, and based upon his Canadian records and reputation that had followed him south of the border, Smith felt that he would make a good fit on the *Wheeling Jamboree*. He asked Hank if he could start right away, and he accepted right then and there, thinking this was the big break he had been hoping for.

Hank kicked off New Year's Day 1945, by making his first appearance on WWVA, from 2:30 to 3:30 P.M. He was back on the air later that same night at 11:30 for another half-hour show. Although he was thrilled about finally making it at WWVA, which meant steady work, it was his appearance on the *Saturday Night Jamboree* that most excited him. Held at the Capitol Theatre in Wheeling, the *Jamboree* performers went on the air in front of a live audience every Saturday night. Hank often said there were no words to describe how he felt when he took that stage for that first time, but he did say that he felt right at home in front of that live audience.

With his spot on the *Jamboree* and regular airtime on the radio, Hank now had a good, stable income, but more importantly he was gaining wider exposure, reaching beyond the Maritimes and even Canada. However, he felt he needed more if he was going to sell his records in the U.S. Along with the radio work, Hank began making personal appearances around Wheeling. Soon the Snows moved out of the Wheeling Hotel and into an apartment.

Knowing of his interest in horses, Slim told Hank about an available horse that he believed would be just right for him. He suggested that Hank buy the animal and keep it at his stables, where he could visit as often as he wanted. Although he didn't know how he was going to get into the horse business, the idea intrigued Hank. Thinking that Slim just might be onto something, Hank wrote to the horse's owner, Elmer Newman, at his ranch near Philadelphia. Hank was excited when he learned the horse was not only reasonably priced, but also came with a background in show business and was capable of doing some extraordinary things. It sounded perfect.

Hank has said that the day Shawnee arrived at Slim's stables was, alongside his marriage to Minnie and the birth of his son, one of the happiest days of his life. Born in Shawnee, Oklahoma—thus the name—the chestnut-and-white-coloured horse was just the right size for Hank. He fell in love with that horse the first minute he laid eyes on him.

With Slim's encouragement, support, and training, and with Shawnee as his partner, Hank set about learning to do stunt riding and rope tricks, skills he planned to incorporate into his act. Training went well and Hank quickly picked up the routine. Eventually, Slim proposed that he and Hank put together a show and go on tour. He further suggested that if Hank wanted to take his show back to the Maritimes, he would be more than happy to help him organize it and then go out on the road with him. Together, with their horses, Slim felt they could put on quite a spectacle, giving the people a show they had never seen before.

The proposal was intriguing to Hank. The idea of showing the folks back home what he had already accomplished in such a short time really appealed to him. And honestly, Hank confessed, both he and Minnie were excited at the prospect of returning home to see the friends and family they deeply missed. However, it would take more

Hank and Shawnee on parade in the mid-1940s.

than a year to mount the effort, as there was a great deal to be done if they were going to pull this off. First, they had to secure financial backing, then they had to find all the necessary equipment needed for such an undertaking. The type of travelling show Slim proposed would be expensive. Such a major production would require a portable grandstand, power generator, lights, trucks, and a horse trailer. But Hank liked the idea, and once he got onto something, he didn't give up easily.

First, Hank had to learn the skills of trick riding. He practised for months, and with Slim's help he was soon performing the stunts as well as a master horseman. Slim encouraged him and said he was a natural. Hank and Shawnee quickly formed an unbreakable bond, an important aspect of the performance as horse and rider had to trust each other and many of the stunts were dangerous if not done properly. Hank often said that the horse understood and performed as if it were human, and their mutual respect was uncanny. It was like the horse could anticipate his next move, Hank said, a quality that made for a successful partnership.

Hank Snow standing in front of the car he used to promote his show with Shawnee.

Upon completing his first stint at the *Jamboree* in the spring of 1945, Hank and his family headed back to Moncton for the summer to put their show plans into effect. The first major challenge was getting Shawnee into Canada, an effort that took careful planning and

Hank and Shawnee spending quality time together in New Brunswick, August 1945.

coordination as the horse required proper vaccinations and papers before crossing the border. Hank also had to build a proper shipping stall to ensure that Shawnee could be sent ahead by train to Moncton while the family travelled by car.

Once in New Brunswick, Hank set about finding everything he needed for the show he hoped to stage the following year. He hired contractors to build his grandstand as well as a horse trailer to haul with his Buick. That summer, once he had planning underway for the following year's spectacle, he hit the road promoting his show as "Hank Snow and his famous horse, Shawnee." It was a huge hit, with audiences responding warmly not just to him, but also to his performing horse, while whetting their appetites for what was to come. It was another major step forward for Hank Snow.

Cowboys and Actors

Hank learned that it would cost roughly six thousand dollars to build everything he would need to go on the road the following summer. Those plans included a grandstand that could be broken down, moved, and reassembled, along with a nine-piece stage, posts for the canvas sidewalls required to keep non-payers from seeing the show, a lighting plant, and ticket booth. If he could raise the money, the contractor assured Hank he could have it all ready for the 1946 summer tour. The price was the obstacle.

Hank had managed to save $1,200 from his radio and stage work in Wheeling, but he needed more money. Banking on his previous success with RCA Victor, Hank boldly wrote to A. H. Joseph, proposing that the record company loan him $4,000 to help finance his equipment and to cover the expenses of bringing Big Slim to Canada for the shows in the summer of 1946. It was a gamble, but he knew no other way to raise the required capital.

Joseph promptly informed Hank that, banking on his earlier success with RCA Victor, the record company executives had agreed to the cash advance. With the financial backing of his record company, Hank then set about ordering the supplies, coordinating the construction of his trucks, stage, and trailers, and overseeing the entire process while considering heading back to West Virginia for the winter, where he hoped to continue working and building his reputation in the U.S. and earn more cash that he could put toward the shows. By the end of the summer of 1945, Hank had wrapped up his theatre tour and headed to Montreal for another recording session. From there, the Snow family returned to Wheeling even though Hank was not assured of work at the station, but after his success the previous winter, he felt good about the prospects.

The hardest thing for Hank at this point was leaving Shawnee in Moncton for the winter, but it made more sense to board him there rather than to haul the animal back across the border to Virginia and then back to New Brunswick again six months later. As much as he loved the horse, the paperwork alone wasn't worth the headache. But Hank wasn't about to leave his prized horse just anywhere. After searching the Moncton area, Hank eventually found a place where he felt Shawnee would be safe and comfortable.

In December 1945, with his plans for the following summer underway and Shawnee in a secure place, Hank and the family went on to Montreal for a two-day recording session during which he cut one of his all-time favourite songs, "My Mother," a tribute to his own mother, as well as future Hank Snow classics "Just a Faded Petal from a Beautiful Bouquet" and "Brand on My Heart."

With the recordings complete, the Snows headed across the border to Wheeling on December 18, with Hank still believing he would land a job once he got there. He was disappointed when he learned that WWVA could not use him as they had already filled their slots in the lineup, but Big Slim suggested he should check out WJPA, a smaller station in nearby Washington, Pennsylvania.

Following Slim's suggestion, Hank headed to Washington, and Bob Clemente, the station manager at WJPA, hired him right away based on his reputation from the previous year at WWVA. He immediately put Hank to work, and offered to make him the station's headliner for the entire winter. Hank took Clemente's offer with the understanding that he could leave without penalty if he found another job that would further his career. Hank went on the air at WJPA every morning at seven o'clock for half an hour, Monday through Friday.

Although WJPA was a smaller station with a more limited range than the much larger WWVA, Hank was grateful for the experience he had there. He also took advantage of his time at WJPA to plan his Maritime tour for the following summer, often travelling back to Wheeling to meet Big Slim, who provided him advice and guidance on how to mount such a major show: it was going to be a massive undertaking, unlike anything the region had ever seen.

Despite the job at WJPA and all the effort he was putting into his Canadian tour, Hank soon became restless. It may have been impulsive, even considered a long shot by those who knew him, but Hank suddenly got the idea that he should go to Hollywood and seek the fame of cowboy movie legends like Gene Autry and Roy Rogers. He knew it wouldn't be easy, but when Hank Snow got something in his head, he wasn't about to let go of the idea. And so, with Minnie's support—and with she and Jimmie settled with some close friends—Hank packed up his car and headed for Hollywood.

Once he arrived, Hank planned to meet a fellow Canadian with whom he had been corresponding in recent months, an actor named Allen Erwin who went by the name "The Calgary Kid," and had played small parts in several Westerns. After a trip that lasted several weeks, and included prolonged visits with new friends he made along the way, Hank arrived in Hollywood, found a cheap hotel room on Western Avenue, and set about his business. Erwin had agreed to show Hank around Hollywood and to take him to all the well-known hot spots where he felt Hank would have the best exposure and maybe even have the chance to meet a few celebrities or people who could help him in his quest to become a movie star.

Although Hank's ultimate dream was to become a singing cowboy in movies like some of his idols, he also knew it would be a difficult dream to fulfill on such short notice, particularly since he wasn't prepared to relocate to Hollywood on a prolonged basis. As promised, Erwin showed Hank around Hollywood and introduced him to producers and industry insiders, while cautioning him not to get his hopes up: breaking into the movie business was difficult and took time.

On one of their excursions, Erwin took Hank to Santa Monica, where he introduced him to legendary entertainer Spade Cooley. Known as "the King of the Western Swing," Cooley led a band that played at an eighteen-thousand-person ballroom. During that visit, Cooley allowed Hank to perform a song with the band. He sang the classic "Molly Darling" that night and was overwhelmed by the audience's reception. It was his largest live audience up to that point.

Making sure that Hank hit all the hot spots for maximum exposure, Erwin took him to the Painted Post, one of the best-known Western-themed nightclubs in Hollywood at the time, as well as Republic Studios, home to some of the legendary Western actors, including Randolph Scott, Roy Rogers, Gabby Hayes, and the Sons of the Pioneers, which, at that time, included Ken Curtis, who went on to play Festus in the long-running television series *Gunsmoke*.

Through Erwin's connections, Hank met a long list of popular celebrities of the era, including Dick Foran, Rod Cameron, Sunset Carson, Lon Chaney Jr., Gene Autry, and Ernie Brewer, some of whom would later play a role in Hank's career. Brewer, for instance, was a famous songwriter whose best-known hit was the novelty song, "Does the Spearmint Lose Its Flavor on the Bedpost Overnight." Hank would later record two of Brewer's songs: "I Knew We'd Meet Again Someday" and "Chattin' With a Chick in Chattanooga."

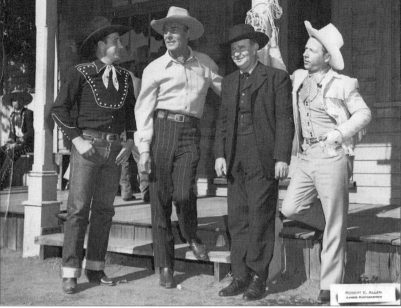

Far right: Hank Snow in Hollywood in 1947. Legendary film actor Randolph Scott is pictured second from left along with actor Gabby Hayes, next to Hank, and an unidentified actor on the far left.

Erwin also took Hank to meet Nathan Turk, Hollywood tailor to the stars, and Hank ordered two suits from him. Later on, whenever Hank needed a new suit, he could place his order from anywhere in the country, as Turk kept his clients' measurements on file. Erwin also took him to meet famed saddle maker Edward H. Bohlin, from whom Hank ordered a new silver saddle and spurs for Shawnee, even though he had no idea how he was going to pay for them. Fortunately, Bohlin agreed to make them on credit. Hank knew Shawnee would sparkle in his new gear.

After spending several weeks in Hollywood, Hank headed back to Pennsylvania. He tried to keep a positive outlook on the adventure: even though he had not broken into the movies, he'd made many important contacts. He also knew that at some point in the future he would be coming back to Hollywood with plans on staying longer, but for now, his family was in Pennsylvania and he had a Canadian tour to organize.

The Summers of 1946 and 1947

In March 1946, Hank and his family headed back to the Maritimes to begin final preparations for the tour. He was both excited and anxious. Although he hoped for success, Hank knew this was a huge and costly risk. He had a lot riding on this investment. If the shows failed, he'd be hard-pressed to repay his record company's loan and he didn't want to jeopardize that relationship and possibly undo everything he had worked so hard to create.

By April, much of Hank's equipment was nearing completion and he felt things were falling into place. With posters printed and venues lined up throughout the Maritimes, he was ready to tour the same region in which he had struggled to scrape out a living only a few years earlier. He was nervous at the prospect of returning to his old stomping grounds, and he wondered how audiences would receive him. He wouldn't have to wonder for long.

Along with Minnie and Jimmie, the backup band, which was comprised mostly of singers and musicians he had worked with in Pennsylvania, Big Slim and his wife Hazel, Shawnee, and the crew, Hank Snow finally hit the road for the first major production of his career. The first performance of Hank's travelling road show was in May 1946 in Moncton. He chose that location to debut the show because he knew the area and felt comfortable there. More importantly, he felt he knew the audience.

By all accounts the tour was a tremendous success. The show, which ran between two and two and a half hours, featured a variety of musical numbers by Hank, Slim, and the band, as well as a number of comedy skits. Even young Jimmie took to the stage for several songs and ultimately became a favourite with the audience. But the indisputable highlight of the show was Hank's routine with Shawnee, in which he would perform the many tricks he had learned from Slim along with others he had perfected on his own, like flipping from the horse's back and landing to his feet on the ground as Shawnee maintained his gallop.

They took the show to various locations throughout the Maritimes and it went on with great success for about three weeks, until Big Slim suddenly informed Hank that he was heading back to

Hank, The Singing Ranger, and Shawnee.

West Virginia—immediately. Slim did not offer an explanation for the abrupt decision, but he announced that Hazel and their animals were going with him, as well as one of the female backup singers. This left Hank in a quandary: he had spent thousands of dollars preparing for this tour, including having posters printed that featured Big Slim, Hazel, and their horses, and now one of his headline acts was pulling out.

Hank never learned what prompted Slim to leave the tour, but he was determined that the show would go on, with everyone else doing double duty. He even expanded Jimmie's role in the lineup, and despite the loss of a featured performer, the audience response was encouraging. As Hank was fond of saying, "the show went on," thanks to the generous folks in Canada, the same people who had supported him throughout his entire career. With a bit of creative ingenuity and tweaking, Hank and his band reworked the lineup and kept the tour going.

Jimmie Rodgers Snow remembers the tour well.

> I travelled with Dad from the time I was born until I was twenty-two. I actually started singing when I was three, and I have particularly strong memories from 1945 to 1946, when I was twelve and I travelled with Dad, Mother, his horse, and two dogs in a horse van with a tent where he would do his shows. I have fond memories of doing the show in Bridgewater at the exhibition grounds in the same place where it is still held today and where they've been holding the tribute [from 1998 to 2012].

For Hank, a highlight on the tour was a stop in Liverpool, just down the road from Brooklyn, where he was born and where he spent much of his early childhood. It had been a few years since he had been back and there was some trepidation on his part about returning, but he knew his mother and sisters would be waiting to watch him perform. It had been a while since he had seen his family and he was anxious to show them everything he had accomplished while he was away.

Unfortunately, despite eventually putting on a successful show for the hometown audience, the event did have some problems. Unbeknownst to Hank, the portable grandstand had been erected on soft, swampy land, and as people were piling in just minutes before the show, the structure collapsed under the weight, pinning several audience members underneath.

Jimmie Snow remembers those summers of 1946 and 1947 with mixed emotions.

> Although these early times on the road were sometimes sad days for someone as young I was, there were

also still some good times in between. I remember Dad bought a semi-truck after saving up money through much sacrifice. This truck had multiple uses. It could carry à big grandstand able to seat five hundred people. The truck was able to carry that grandstand and all of our equipment as well, and it also served as our stage to perform from. Once it was set up, Dad would do trick riding and put Shawnee through a series of tricks. As a child I remember singing to those audiences from that stage. Another picture that stands out in my mind is of one time when the grandstand collapsed and fell. I remember a lot of people were injured seriously, but somehow or another we managed to survive the ordeal with no great cost to Dad. It was at this point Dad decided to get rid of all this gear and move in another direction with his career.

Although Hank had reservations about proceeding with the performance, the hometown crowd pushed for him to continue. Ultimately he did not want to disappoint those who came to see him. Although embarrassed that the incident was reported in the papers, Hank would come to learn that as a successful entertainer, everything he did would be under public scrutiny.

Despite the occasional bad luck, Hank deemed the tour of 1946 an overwhelming success. After travelling throughout much of the Maritimes for two months, the show wrapped up in New Brunswick and the band members headed home. After paying the bills and ensuring all the equipment was safely stored for the winter, the Snows made their way back to Washington, Pennsylvania, where Hank could reassess his career and set a course for his next big venture. Things had moved quickly for him in recent years and he felt it was time to determine where he was going from here.

Once he was back in the states and sure that Minnie and Jimmie were settled again, Hank headed to Philadelphia to meet Jack Howard. He hoped Jack would be able to help him line up a band to accompany him to Canada in the summer of 1947, as many of the former members had confirmed they would not be going back.

Hank and his gang touring the Maritimes in 1946.

They found that, on top of performing, the routine of travelling and helping to put up and take down the equipment was too taxing. Luckily, Howard introduced Hank to a trio of talented western singers who agreed to join him on his Canadian tour the following summer. Soon, the deal was set, complete with legal contracts. Hank thought all the details were locked down, but like with everything else in life—and especially in the entertainment business—nothing is ever for sure, and legal contracts are only as good as the people who sign them; a lesson Hank would learn the hard way.

After spending a number of weeks with Howard in Philadelphia, during which time he visited several radio stations and had meetings with music industry executives, Hank returned to Washington, Pennsylvania, where he spent the winter of 1946 planning the next summer's tour. In the spring of 1947, Hank and his family returned to Moncton to make final preparations. He went to the same dealership where he had purchased the Buick in 1945 and ordered a brand new, 1947 canary-yellow Cadillac convertible, complete with automatic transmission and power steering. (Today, this car can be seen at the Hank Snow Home Town Museum in Liverpool.) He made arrangements to take ownership of the vehicle after the tour was complete in the fall. By late spring, the trio from Philadelphia arrived and Hank put them up in a local motel. After several rehearsals, Hank believed they were ready to hit the road.

Wanting to expand his territory during this tour, Hank had booked shows further afield in Ontario and Quebec, places he had not previously played. He knew this was a gamble. Other than an occasional show on the national CBC network, Hank had no prior exposure in these areas, but that did not deter him, as he felt it was time to expand his reach. Besides, he was used to gambling and he felt he was ready to expand. But there would be a few hitches, as there usually are.

Although Hank believed he had hired a trustworthy band, it turned out the trio from Philadelphia was anything but reliable. When it came time to leave for Montreal, Hank was surprised to learn that the musicians had already left Moncton. Even though the plan had been for the entire company to travel together, Hank hoped they had gone on ahead and that they would meet him at the RCA Victor building in Montreal, the first stop on their tour. However, upon arriving in Montreal, where he met with A. H. Joseph, Hank was disappointed to find that the trio had not arrived.

A day later, after arriving in Ottawa where they were scheduled to perform, Hank learned that the three men had returned to the U.S. This posed a major problem for Hank. Not only did this leave him without a backup band but it also left him with a supply of posters and other promotional materials, including pictures of the trio. But just like the summer before when Big Slim had bailed on him, Hank would not let this development get him down. Instead, he contacted several musicians he knew in the Maritimes, hired them, and brought them to Ottawa to join the tour. He then quickly reorganized the show lineup to once again feature more performances by Jimmie and Shawnee.

The show went on, and was a huge success. Even though his audiences in Ontario and Quebec were small, Hank felt that was largely because he wasn't as well known in the region. He was also content with the response, for the most part, and he made enough money to pay his bills and cover the band's salaries, his top priorities. Upon wrapping up the Ontario and Quebec legs of the tour, the show returned to familiar ground in the Maritimes and immediately drew larger crowds throughout the remainder of the summer.

With the summer tour complete, the group returned to Moncton and Hank made plans for the winter. This time, he would take Shawnee with him instead of leaving him in Moncton. While still winding up his tour business, Hank had decided his ultimate destination was Hollywood and, since he was planning on an extended stay, he did not want to leave the horse behind.

Although in many ways Hank considered the summer tours of 1946 and 1947 successful ventures, he had had enough of the hectic road shows. Considering some of the challenges he had faced in mounting the shows, he sold everything except the horse trailer and van, which he would need to haul Shawnee and the family's personal belongings (and the capitol from which he needed to get to Hollywood).

It was at that time that Hank received an invitation from a DJ at a radio station in Tacoma, Washington, who had been playing his records for several years. The DJ told Hank that he had developed a substantial fan base in the region and encouraged him to come to the West Coast for some personal appearances. Hank felt that this move would help promote his music and so, with Minnie's support, he accepted the invitation and finalized plans for the trip. Minnie and Jimmie would remain in Moncton and Hank would send for them once he got settled.

NEVER SAY QUIT

Go West, Young Man

His *plans were* set, but as he was preparing to leave for the West Coast, Hank received notice from the American Federation of Musicians that the Philadelphia trio was suing him for breach of contract, even though, after allowing Hank to pick up all their expenses while they were in Moncton, they'd skipped town without doing one performance and left him with a substantial gap in the show. Although Hank was angered by their audacity, he was hurt more than anything. He learned the hard way that not everyone could be trusted. Regrettably, it was a lesson he would learn many times throughout his life.

Instead of seeking legal advice to settle this dispute as he should have done, Hank attempted to deal with the matter on his own, a decision that would later come back to haunt him. He was hurt and frustrated by the trio's actions, but for now, he believed the matter was settled and he was heading west on the invitation of Buck Ritchey, the DJ in Tacoma. Before departing, however, Hank went to Montreal for a brief recording session at RCA Victor. From December 2 to 5, 1947, he recorded twelve new songs for the label, including the country classics, "Wasted Love," "Somewhere Along Life's Highway," and "My Two-Timin' Woman."

After a quick return to Moncton to make sure Minnie and Jimmie were settled with friends, Hank was ready to make his second trip to Hollywood, and this time, determined to make it there, he vowed to stay as long as it took. With the help of a van driver he had hired in Moncton, Hank's things were packed and the horse trailer was prepared for the journey. Not really sure what he would find on the West Coast, but hoping this was another important step in his career, he headed out on his new adventure. After several days of practically non-stop driving, he arrived, setting up camp on a vacant grassy lot adjacent to Ventura Boulevard, as he needed someplace to exercise Shawnee every day. With the landowner's permission—and agreement to look after the animal while Hank was away during the day—Hank could go about his business while being sure his prized horse was comfortable and safe.

Hank spent the next few weeks putting out feelers and making contact with people in the music and movie businesses. In time, he found his way to MCA (Music Corporation of America), which, after listening to his records, agreed to put him under contract. He also ended up at the Frank Foster Booking Agency, which took him on as a client but recommended he get a band if he wanted to play in live venues. Hank did just that and pulled together a western swing band to back him while he prepared to tour Washington and Oregon. After rehearsing for several weeks, making plans, and doing occasional dances, Hank was ready to hit the road once gain. He was anxious to do major shows with his band and hoped Foster would come through with some tour dates—and quickly, he needed a cash infusion to cover his living expenses, buy feed for Shawnee, pay for advertising as suggested by Foster, and to pay his band, all of which didn't come cheap.

Desperate for money, Hank tried to sell the U.S. rights to his songs to music publishers in Hollywood, but at first had no luck finding a buyer as publishers felt there was little market for his style of music. Never one to be easily dissuaded, Hank eventually made his way to the offices of Hill and Range Songs, Inc., a publishing company owned by brothers Julian and Jean Aberbach, and made his plea, outlining his earlier success and pitching his brand of music. After considering the pitch, Julian anted up one thousand dollars to help cover Hank's expenses, on the condition that he would talk to the brothers about a long-term contract. Hank accepted the offer and in 1948, reciprocating the brothers' kindness, he signed an exclusive writing contract with Hill and Range. It was a deal he would never regret.

Cover of a Hill and Range songbook featuring Hank's songs.

Here was Hank, in Hollywood, on the cusp of what he thought were big things for him with a publishing deal, a booking agent, and lots of enthusiasm. Now, all he needed were show dates to generate much-needed funds. He was desperate and felt trapped. He couldn't even consider heading back to Moncton at that point—he had no money to put gas in the car. To hold him over until he had a steady income and to avoid borrowing more money from friends, Hank did the only thing he could think of: he took out a three thousand-dollar loan at the Vine and Sunset Company, using his van and all his equipment as collateral. From that loan, he sent money back to Minnie in Moncton to help tide her over, and he paid some of the bills he had accumulated since arriving in Hollywood, including money owed to the members of his band, who were starting to get antsy. He also gave a portion of the money to Foster for advertising and publicity photos; he knew that, as an up-and-coming entertainer, it was important that he be seen in the large trade papers. While it was an expensive proposition even in those days, it was the only way to generate a buzz, something Hank had to do as an unknown singer in a community swarming with other entertainers. The competition was stiff, even at that time.

With such expenses, it wasn't long, however, before the loan was gone and Vine and Sunset was demanding payment. Since he didn't have the money to pay on the debt, Hank considered his options, one of which was fleeing Hollywood and leaving his debts behind. With things hitting a brick wall on the West Coast, he considered going to Dallas, Texas, and pursing his options there, especially since he had been corresponding with a promoter named Bea Terry from Greenville, Texas. She told him that a Dallas radio station, KRLD, had somehow gotten hold of his Canadian records and was playing them in steady rotation. As a result, the records were becoming big hits in the Dallas area and she encouraged Hank to come there to support their success.

Hank determined that he should be in Dallas when he learned that his song, "Brand on My Heart," had held the number one position in Texas for sixteen consecutive weeks. KRLD was a ten thousand-watt AM station with considerable reach throughout the mid and southern U.S. If Hank's records were doing well there, it was a huge boost to his career. Rolling the dice once again and wanting to get out of California while he could, Hank let his band go, packed up his things, and headed to Dallas.

Hank eventually learned that Betty Goudie, one of his loyal Canadian friends, had sent his records to KRLD. Although Betty lived in Victoria, British Columbia, she became a major promoter of his music, which was dominating the Canadian airwaves by that time. Betty had joined the Hank Snow Fan Club, which Hank had launched in Moncton a few years earlier as a way to raise funds. He charged one dollar for a membership, and he and Minnie would send out a small newsletter every three months with news about upcoming shows, records, and tours. Minnie, who wrote under the name "Queenie Dalhurt," was the editor.

Jimmie Rodgers Snow recalled the events from this time with mixed emotions. "I remember when Dad left us to go to Hollywood to try and further his career. He thought it might be possible if he could get connected with the Hollywood scene with all the cowboy Westerns that were dominating the big screen at that time. It was the era of the singing cowboy—Tex Ritter, Gene Autry, Roy Rogers, Eddie Dean and so on."

But, as with many other ventures his father tried in those earlier days of his career, nothing went according to plan: "Dad lost all the money he had saved up, and I'm not sure how it happened, but he eventually wound up in the nightclub scene in Dallas, Texas."

Once established in the new territory, Hank sent for his family to join him. He was greatly disappointed about his lack of success on the West Coast, but based upon this early response to his records on the radio, he had bigger hopes for Texas.

The Lone Star State

Once in Dallas, Hank set up camp and then went about exploring the possibilities awaiting him in the city. Never once did he think that he should just pack up and move back home. It wasn't an option. He had fought hard his entire life to realize his dreams and he felt he had reached the point where he could not turn back.

From Dallas, Hank made his way to Greenville to meet Bea Terry, the woman who had encouraged him to come to the Lone Star State. It was thrilling for him to hear his songs being played on U.S. radio stations for the first time, and through Bea's connections, Hank hit the radio circuit in Dallas, doing interviews and performing wherever the opportunity arose, but mostly at record stores. Through those efforts, he received his first big break in Texas.

Hank and Shawnee performing outside the Roundup Club in Dallas, Texas, in 1948.

After only a few days in the state, Steve Stephens, owner of a Dallas nightclub called the Roundup Club, offered Hank a job, which he immediately accepted. He earned $250 for a two-week stint where he played two shows daily, seven days a week, one at 9:00 P.M. and again at 11:00 P.M. With the club's house band providing backup, Hank was an instant hit with the audience, and Stephens signed him on for an additional two weeks under the same terms. With his songs playing on Texas radio stations combined with a steady, albeit short-term job, Hank was anxious to move his music career forward, but remained guardedly optimistic about his budding success.

Within a short time, people were asking for Hank's records wherever he went, but the singer was not aware they were being sold in the U.S. However, Hank soon discovered that A. H. Joseph in Montreal had made a deal with Steve Sholes, the new head of RCA Victor in New York, to slowly release some of Hank's records into the American market on a limited trial basis, especially in Texas. Country music was big in the southern region, and RCA executives felt that if his records had a chance in the country that would be the place for it to happen.

With the help of Don Snellings, a sales representative for Adleda Records, RCA's Texas distributor, Hank hit the circuit with a new determination, promoting his music and doing interviews. Through these appearances, he met fans and radio DJs, signed autographs, and sang wherever and whenever an opportunity presented itself. During this time, while living a meagre existence, he saved as much money as he could spare to bring his family to Texas.

Although he continued to do shows at the Roundup Club, whenever there was an opening for him, Hank also did shows at other clubs throughout the region, including one spot called the Silver Spur, owned by the infamous Jack Ruby. (Yes, the same Jack Ruby who shot Lee Harvey Oswald.) While history portrays Ruby as a killer with possible mob connections, Hank always insisted he had a good relationship with the seemingly seedy nightclub owner. It is possible that Hank only saw the good side of Ruby, the man who allowed him to play in his place on several occasions, part-time work that Hank was desperate to accept.

Even though he was struggling to get out from under the financial burdens that he felt were getting in the way of his creative drive, Hank managed to save sufficient funds to bring his family to the United States. Jimmie recalled how excited his mother was at finally getting the word from Hank that it was time for them to come to Texas. He also remembered boarding a train in Halifax and heading to the U.S. to meet up with his father in Dallas. In particular, he remembers how excited he was when the train passed through Boston as they headed for what his mother told him would be a new adventure.

> It was quite an ordeal when Mother and I crossed the border and entered the United States of America. It was 1948 in the month of December when we made our way by train all the way from Halifax to Port Huron, Michigan, and then on to Dallas, Texas. It was a week by train and very difficult and tough on Mother and I.... We had no idea what kind of life waited for us down there, but it had been a while since we had seen Dad, so we were anxious to get there.

Hank, Jimmie, who was now twelve years old, and Minnie, inside their Lovett Avenue house in Dallas.

Minnie and Jimmie arrived in Dallas on December 18, 1948, and with his family now beside him, Hank finally felt he could settle down. Finding a place that he could afford and that could also accommodate Shawnee proved to be a challenge, however. Early in 1949, the family found a small place in south Dallas on Lovett Avenue. The three-room apartment cost them sixty dollars a month, money Hank didn't have. With the help of a friend, however, Hank managed

Early promotional postcard for Hank, the Blue Yodelling Ranger. This photo is from CKCW in Moncton.

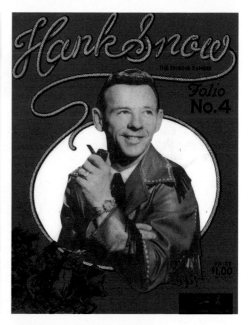

Covers of Hill and Range songbooks, featuring Hank's songs.

Hank in his office at Rainbow Ranch.

The Snow home in Madison, known as Rainbow Ranch.

The barn Hank had built at Rainbow Ranch for Shawnee.

Hank and Shawnee pose at Rainbow Ranch.

Hank Snow and the Rainbow Ranch Boys in front of an early tour bus.

Hank and Elvis backstage at the Grand Ole Opry, January 1958.

Hank Snow in 1971.

Hank Snow on stage in Bridgewater in August 1982.

Hank Snow at the Country Music Hall of Fame in Nashville.

Hank's guitar.

Statue of Hank Snow in Nashville.

to pull together enough to cover the first month's rent, but things weren't looking good. The Snows were broke and Hank had nothing lined up. The Roundup Club was fully booked and he couldn't find work anywhere else.

Nearly destitute, the early days on Lovett Avenue were difficult for the Snows. At one point, they went without food for three days. Although Hank was still driving his Cadillac—as Jimmie recalled, image was important to his father even when he was struggling—he soon ran out of money to buy gas, so transportation was also limited. Desperate to raise money, Hank sold a few personal belongings, including a ring that held sentimental value to him, and raised five hundred dollars, which he used to pay off bills and to buy household supplies. But nothing was ever easy for Hank, and at this point the loan company from Hollywood had managed to track him down in Dallas. When they caught up with him, they demanded payment on his outstanding loan, threatening to repossess his horse trailer and van, and possibly even the silver saddle he'd had made for Shawnee during his first trip to California. Hank wasn't about to let that happen, and with the help of several friends, he secured a second loan from a Dallas-based company and used it to pay off the first debt.

He may have held the hounds at bay for a short while, but Hank was far from out of the woods. For someone in Hank's position, however, time was an important ally, because as he struggled, he also continued to believe he was on the verge of something major. It was close—he felt it, he believed it. Despite these hardships, Hank continued to believe his big break was just around the corner. Throughout his time in Canada, Hollywood, and Dallas, he had stayed in contact with Ernest Tubb, one of the biggest country music stars in the U.S. at the time. They had connected, by letter, several years earlier, and had a special bond over their love for the music of Jimmie Rodgers. Over the years, the two had exchanged many letters, but they had never personally met. That all changed when Hank was invited to play at the Cowtown Jamboree at the Northside Coliseum, featuring a stellar lineup of country music stars from Nashville, including headliner Ernest Tubb. Not only would Hank earn twenty-five dollars to perform on the show, he would finally get the chance to meet Tubb.

Hank credited Grand Ole Opry star Ernest Tubb with helping to get him to the greatest country music stage of them all.

During that first meeting, as they spent hours talking about Jimmie Rodgers, Tubb encouraged Hank to make his way to Nashville, Tennessee, where the country music scene was exploding. As Tubb was also based there, he told Hank that if he came he would help him get a spot on the Grand Ole Opry, the most famous country music stage in the world. However, to play on the Opry, an artist had to have a hit record, something Hank did not have yet in the U.S. Despite his success in Canada, and even his growing popularity in Texas, it would not be easy to make it to that famous stage. But like everything else in his past, Hank felt an appearance on the Opry was worth fighting for. He knew it would be a long shot, but Tubb promised to do everything he could to help him and it felt good to have someone with that much clout pulling for him.

True to his word, a few days following the Northside Coliseum show, Tubb called to tell Hank he had spoken to Jim Perry, the Opry manager, and Jack Stapp, the program director, about the possibility of Hank performing there and maybe even taking Tubb's spot while he was on tour. Unfortunately, to Hank's disappointment, they couldn't take him at that time because of their hit-record criteria. But Hank would not give up the dream of performing at the Opry someday. For now though, he had be content with what he had going on in Texas, which mostly meant concentrating on finding work and taking care of his family. But despite his struggles, Hank never lost sight of the bigger prize: a spot on the Grand Ole Opry stage.

While filling in occasionally at the Roundup Club, Hank was introduced to Lucky Moeller, an acclaimed entertainer from the region who was the leader of a western-style swing band. Moeller had heard of the singing cowboy from Canada who had been making waves in Texas of late, and because of that reputation, he offered Hank a job touring with his band for ten days throughout Texas and Oklahoma. Moeller would pay Hank twenty-five dollars a night for singing and playing with the band as well as expenses. Hank quickly took the offer; the money was a big boost at a time when things were desperate.

Around this same time, Hank also heard of the *Louisiana Hayride* that was held in Shreveport, Louisiana, and broadcast every Saturday night over a fifty thousand-watt AM station. It sounded like another good opportunity to him. Finding out that a man named Frank Page booked talent for *The Hayride*, Hank called and asked if they could use him on the show. Because of Hank's reputation, Page invited him to send along some records for him to listen to. He told Hank that once he had the records he would get back in touch. Two weeks after Hank's initial call, he landed a performance for himself and Shawnee on *The Hayride*. The job paid $125 for the night, extremely good money in those times—and a welcome, if temporary, reprieve from the financial woes that continued to dog him.

Despite all these efforts and opportunities he created for himself in Texas, Hank knew that any significant future success in the country music business would only come when he had his records released throughout the U.S. To that end, both he and Joseph in Montreal had been trying to convince Sholes to bring Hank to New York's RCA studios for a recording session, but Sholes had the final call on who they recorded in the U.S. He would not be swayed by any amount of pressure from either Hank or Joseph.

Finally, though, in March 1949, persistence paid off when Hank was invited to Chicago to record four songs for RCA in the U.S. As part of the deal, Hank agreed that he would record two songs by other writers, and if he had two of his own songs that Sholes felt were strong enough, he could also record those; however, he would have to convince the record producer the songs were worth the effort. The challenge was Hank's to meet, but he knew he was up to the task.

On this trip, Hank planned to bring along a song he had been working on for some time and also playing for some friends. Even though the early response to the song was positive, he was still hesitant about going public with it because he wasn't sure it was polished enough. Despite his nerves and early reservations, however, he felt it was a good song and intended to suggest it as one of his two compositions. Its working title: "I'm Movin' On."

Once in Chicago, Hank, along with Minnie and Jimmie, who had accompanied him on the trip, met with Sholes at the Edgewater Beach Hotel to discuss the songs he would record. Also at the meeting were bass player Charlie Greon, and Al Gallico, a young publishing executive who, at the time, was just starting his own music company. On the strength of some of Hank's songs, Gallico eventually turned his venture into one of the biggest music companies in the U.S., but for now the recording session was the immediate concern, and the men wanted to hear what Hank could do.

However, when Hank performed "I'm Movin' On," neither Sholes or Greon liked it well enough to approve it for the session. Naturally, Hank was disappointed by their decision, but although he believed Sholes had passed on a great song, he chose not to argue the point, instead embracing the opportunity he had fought for. On March 8, 1949, over the course of three hours, Hank recorded his first songs in the U.S., including "Marriage Vow," penned by legendary songwriter Jenny Lou Carson, and "(I Wished Upon) My Little Horseshoe." When the session was over, Hank returned to Dallas, where he was told to sit tight and wait for word from Sholes. He had learned long ago that a big part of the music business was having the patience to wait. At that point, he had no idea what was going to happen next, but within two weeks, Sholes informed Hank that RCA would be releasing "Marriage Vow" for his first U.S. record, and the flip side would be "Star Spangled Waltz," a song Hank had written while driving to Chicago, and now considered by many to be one of his best compositions.

Kayton Roberts, one of two remaining members of Hank's band, The Rainbow Ranch Boys, as of 2013, said that of all of Hank's songs, "Star Spangled Waltz" is his favourite.

"It's a beautiful love song," he said, recalling that Hank "wrote that song on his way to Chicago to go to his first recording session in the U.S. He just wrote the song off the cuff and it was lovely. You can tell it came naturally as the lyrics aren't forced and the melody is simple, but inspired. It's the most beautiful song I think I've ever heard."

Despite feeling good about the songs he had recorded for Sholes and believing that he had done the best he could, Hank worried if the record would sell, but for now things were out of his hands. Not a patient man, Hank knew waiting to see how the Americans responded to his music would be tough, but he couldn't dwell on that. He had more pressing concerns to worry about as he was still trying to survive in Dallas and struggling to support his family.

Thankfully, Hank was getting the occasional job at the Roundup Club, and when Steve Stephens decided to open a second Dallas location, he assured Hank that he could get more work there. But with the bills continuing to pile up and no prospects of steady employment, Hank felt it was time to make another big move.

Back to Canada

Even though things were starting to happen for Hank, in Dallas with the nightclub shows and the RCA recording session in Chicago, they weren't happening fast enough. The family was still financially strapped and struggling to make ends meet, so Hank felt it was time to do something drastic to change things up, and hopefully propel him further along his career path. He decided to return to Canada for another tour that would, once and for all, establish him as a national recording artist in his native country. Despite having some success in Canada with earlier recordings and smaller regional tours, he felt he had not yet fully tapped into the potentially larger Canadian audience, and so it was that he decided to head north of the border and back to the land of his birth.

In Canada, Hank's plan was to start on the West Coast and, once established there, cross the country, playing and singing as he went. It was an ambitious plan—especially in an era when transportation wasn't what it is today, and with no money to cover such an elaborate tour—but Hank felt it was the right time to stir things up once again.

Hank and Shawnee as they headed back to Canada.

In May 1949, Hank and his family headed to New Westminster, British Columbia, where Hank planned to start his journey. There he met with Bill Ray, the manager at radio station CKNW, to discuss his planned tour. As with earlier shows, Hank knew it was important to get support from people in the radio industry, people who understood what the audience would expect from him during such a tour and could promote him on the air. Based on Hank's reputation, Ray immediately gave him a job singing with the staff band. The Snows decided to make New Westminster their home until Hank could figure out his next move. Although he longed for the day he could appear on the Grand Ole Opry, Hank had bills to pay and a family to support, so he would continue to work in British Columbia while waiting for word from RCA about how his records were doing and thinking about the next leg of his cross-Canada tour.

And as always, waiting was hard for Hank, a driven man who couldn't sit still for long. To fill the time and earn a few extra dollars, Hank used the station band while he toured throughout British

Columbia, doing shows and attracting large audiences. In fact, the response was so positive toward Hank that Ray, recognizing an opportunity, rented the Vancouver Gardens, a venue that could hold more than seven thousand people, and put on a country music spectacular. He used local talent and featured Hank Snow, The Singing Ranger, and his trick horse, Shawnee, as the headline act. The venue sold out. It was a dream come true for Hank, that he could draw so many people who would come and hear him sing and perform with his trick horse. Spurred on by this success, he continued to tour throughout the Canadian West Coast, expanding his audience and creating an ever-growing fan base.

With his rise in popularity, Hank began planning larger tours. He hired his own musicians and sought other entertainers to add to the lineup. As with his earlier tours of the Maritimes, Hank believed that a larger show featuring a variety of acts, with him as the headliner, would draw bigger audiences. One entertainer Hank wanted in the lineup was Billy King, a world-renowned juggler and tightrope performer he knew from his early days in Lunenburg. He thought Billy's brand of light and fun entertainment would be a good fit for the show and brought him all the way from the East Coast to join the lineup.

For Jimmie, this was a good thing, as he and Billy quickly became close friends. With Hank being so busy with his radio work, lining up shows, practising, promoting, and performing his music, he didn't have much time to spend with his son, so Billy, almost by default, filled the void. Jimmie embraced the friendship.

> It was great having Billy around. Since we didn't stay
> in one place very long, because of Dad's music, I didn't
> have the opportunity to make friends with other kids
> my own age. Billy and me had a lot of fun together...
> [h]e taught me how to juggle...but mostly we just hung
> around together. It was great having someone to chum
> around with. A young boy needs a man around to learn
> from, and with Dad being so busy with the shows, he
> just didn't have the time to spare. I didn't hold that
> against him, though, because I knew how important
> his music was to him.

Years later, Jimmie said he regretted that he and his father had never really had the opportunity to develop a better father-son relationship, but he also accepted that his father's life as an up-and-coming entertainer required his full attention and took most of his energy. Jimmie knew that his father had feelings for him, but he also understood that as a driven man, his father was focused on building his career. "His music was important to him," Jimmie said. "I understood that, but I also know that his family was important to him...it was just that there is only so much one person can do. But he gave me more opportunities growing up than most children could ever imagine. I don't hold anything against him."

The trip to Canada was working well for Hank. Things were finally looking up for him and they were about to get even better: Hank's American publisher, Julian Aberback from Hill and Range Songs in Hollywood, contacted him with news that his good friend Ernest Tubb had just recorded his song "My Filipino Rose," and it would be released in the U.S. on his next record. Naturally, Hank was ecstatic at the news, not because of royalties he would receive as the writer (although the money would be welcomed), but because Tubb, who was then one of the most successful country music artists in the states, had recorded a song he had written, thus cementing their friendship and ensuring that Hank's music would find its way to an ever-expanding audience. It also reassured Hank that with people like Tubb supporting him, a path to the Grand Ole Opry was being cleared for him. He had faith that it would happen some day, but he had work to do in the meantime.

Legendary juggler Billy King from Lunenburg toured Canada with Hank Snow in the late 1940s.

Things had gone well for Hank in British Columbia, but after spending several months there and despite the success he was achieving, he felt it was time to strike out again. He and Minnie followed up on an invitation from Andy Patterson, who operated Patterson's Barn, a popular dance hall in Winnipeg, Manitoba. According to Patterson, Hank was pretty well known in Winnipeg and he felt Hank would do well there. Hank was excited by the prospect of exploring new territory.

The family stayed in Winnipeg for the entire summer, performing at Patterson's Barn, where Hank drew large audiences. Hank had fond memories of his time in Manitoba and felt the reputation he built there as a country music singer had gone a long way to establishing him as a national entertainer. Eventually he decided to move on again, however. He liked it in Winnipeg and although he was tempted to stay, he also knew that for his plans to work it was important to keep reaching out to new audiences.

Jimmie Rodgers Snow remembers this constant touring throughout Canada.

> In the early years, Dad always made it a point to come back home to the Maritimes as often as he could. We played a lot of shows there and we toured across Canada a lot in my younger days. Dad was taking his show out to the audiences so there was no such thing as a permanent home for us. I also remember Mother cooking on a small gas stove on the back of an old truck that was our home for some of the time. It was about one foot by one and a half feet in size. As a matter of fact, I still have that stove to this day. There wasn't a lot of money in those days so we couldn't afford to stay in hotels and at that time, motels didn't exist so there was no going there. I remember that when we were playing a show in Pictou or some other small town in the Maritimes and we needed a place to stay at night, the truck became our only option.

Furthermore, Jimmie says, if they had any money, which wouldn't have been much at that time, his father wouldn't have used it for a place to sleep. "Times were pretty tough for us, as they were for a lot of other people back then. Whenever Dad made any money, he saved it. Early on, he believed that if he was going to make it big he would have to go the United States because they just weren't aware of Nova Scotia and the music coming from there so he had to go to them. He knew it would take money to travel so he saved every penny he could."

By the end of the summer of 1949, Hank, Minnie, and Jimmie, along with Billy King—who was still performing his juggling act during each of Hank's shows—headed east to Hank's old stomping grounds. While Hank had lined up several shows in Ontario and Quebec, he was most anxious to return to the Maritimes. He couldn't wait to get back to the place where his dreams had taken root. This time he also wanted to include stops in Newfoundland, a place he had often visited while on the fishing boats but never as a performer. That had to change if he truly wanted to be considered a national artist. Before leaving Winnipeg, Hank reached out to Mengie Schulman, a DJ he had heard of at CJON in St. John's, Newfoundland, and told him he would be there by early fall. Since Schulman had a good reputation for supporting Canadian talent, Hank wanted him to promote his upcoming visit and then to help with the shows once he got to Newfoundland.

Their first stop in New Brunswick was in Campbellton, where Hank had worked at the radio station several years earlier. There, Hank's old friend Stan Chapman agreed to give him two daily time slots at the station—2:00 P.M. and 7:30 P.M.—while Hank organized his band and prepared for his tour. He could do the shows as long as he wanted. With the help of another old friend, Johnny Beaudoin, in New Carlisle, Quebec, Hank lined up several other musicians and booked shows at some of the same locations he had played years earlier. The tour was a successful effort and Hank was happy with the response he received from the familiar audiences.

After wrapping up his shows in Quebec and New Brunswick, it was off to Nova Scotia. Their first stop in his home province was Halifax, where they stayed with Minnie's family in Fairview. While there, Hank finalized plans for his first tour of Newfoundland. To start, he contacted record store owner Gus Winter in St. John's and learned from him that Hank Snow records were doing very well in Newfoundland and that fans were anxious to see him live. Meanwhile, as Hank was making final arrangements for the tour, he received word that his first U.S. song, "Marriage Vow," was doing well on the charts, news that convinced him that he was on the verge of a major breakthrough in the American market; but for now it was off to Newfoundland. Along with Billy King, Jimmie, and several backup-band members that he had hired from New Brunswick and Nova Scotia, Hank headed to Sydney, Cape Breton, where he caught the ferry to Port aux Basques. He had also made arrangements to board Shawnee at a stable in Sydney, while Minnie stayed with her family in Halifax.

Once in Newfoundland, Hank went to work promoting shows by day and performing with the band at night. At first, audiences were small, but once word got out that Hank Snow was performing live, the numbers swelled. With the help of DJ Mengie Schulman, shows were soon drawing large audiences—the size Hank had become accustomed to. Although the venues were small compared to some of those in which Hank was now used to playing, with the largest hall holding about three hundred and fifty, he still considered the three-week tour to be a success because of the people he met and the contacts he made in Newfoundland. Not only that, but Hank had done what he had set out to do—becoming one of the first entertainers to play music from one coast of Canada to the other.

THE BIG BREAK

From Dallas to Nashville

Back in Halifax, Hank received a letter from Bea Terry telling him that the operator of the Dallas Sportatorium wanted Hank to contact him as quickly as possible. With no way of knowing what was up, but hoping this meant something big was brewing, Hank felt he had to get back right away and immediately made plans to return to Texas. In Dallas, he discovered that a club owner in Fort Worth was putting together a large country show at Corpus Christi and had contacted Fred Edwards, a DJ at station KRLD, about lining up support entertainment. The show's headliner was the legendary Hank Williams, and Edwards was looking to beef up his opening acts. Based on Hank's previous success in Texas and his growing popularity on the radio, the promoter offered him two hundred dollars if he wanted the spot in the lineup. Did he want it?

Hank didn't even have to think about it. Of course he wanted it.

Even in those early years, Hank Williams was a legend in country music circles. Rumours of his heavy drinking had already begun circulating, but Hank Snow always said he found the singer to be open, friendly, and genuinely willing to help him, a struggling artist on his way up. Meeting Hank Williams was a chance Hank could not pass up. While the show was a success, it was the connection the two singer-songwriters made that was more significant to Snow. He believed they hit it off so quickly because they had a great deal in common: they'd both grown up in poverty and performed mostly original material. They'd also both had to scratch their way up the ladder and could appreciate each other's struggles. In short, Hank Snow believed Hank Williams recognized a lot of himself in the Canadian and because of that, their bond was instant and deep, their mutual friendship forged out of respect and understanding.

At their first meeting, Williams offered his unequivocal support and encouraged Snow to come back to *The Louisiana Hayride* as his guest. Hank Snow jumped at the offer to return to the country music show. He thought that his first performance there had gone well, but also knew it would be great exposure for him to be seen at *The Hayride* with Hank Williams, a man who attracted considerable attention wherever he went. With Minnie and Jimmie now settled down in Dallas, Snow made his way to Shreveport, where he was warmly welcomed by Hank Williams and where he performed before audiences that appreciated his music. He always had warm memories of his appearances at the Shreveport venue and credited *The Hayride* for helping him find an American audience.

Following a successful show at *The Hayride*, Snow returned to Dallas feeling that he and Williams had become good friends, but by this time he was getting restless and was anxious to hear from Ernest Tubb and the Grand Ole Opry. While he understood that getting on the Opry was a long shot, he held out hope that his growing reputation and his friendship with Tubb would help to secure him a place on the famous stage. Meanwhile, he had bills to pay so he had to keep working. While waiting for word from the Opry, Hank asked Don Snellings from Adleda Records to continue lining up personal appearances for him, taking him on the radio and record store circuit to promote his records.

When he wasn't working or doing something to promote his music, Hank began visiting the Big D Jamboree at the Dallas auditorium, a hot spot where many of the era's biggest country music stars were appearing. It was there that he met the famed Cowboy Copas, and through him Hank eventually met promoter Oscar Davis, who in future years would go on to promote many of Hank Snow's shows. Despite all this activity, Hank longed to appear on the Opry, where all the major artists of the day were performing. He had paid his dues and put in his time. Now he was waiting for the invitation, and the waiting was the most difficult part of the entertainment business.

Finally, in late 1949, Ernest Tubb called with news that the Opry now had an opening and to tell Hank he should come to Nashville right away. Leaving Minnie and Jimmie in Dallas until he was settled, Hank headed to Nashville. Despite his success in Texas, Hank still didn't have a national hit record, and that fact weighed heavy on him. In truth, he wasn't really sure how he could have gotten the invitation in the first place, because he knew that no one was invited to be a member of the Opry without a hit record. However, the fact that his friend had told him to come to Nashville was encouraging, and he hoped that maybe he would be the exception to the rule. Hank felt he was good enough to play there, but if it didn't happen he'd go back to Dallas and work harder. He liked it in Texas and appreciated the opportunities he had been given there, but he was ready to move on. He hoped this would be the opportunity he had been waiting for.

In Nashville, Hank connected with Tubb, who immediately took him to see Opry manager Jim Denny at the WSM studio on Seventh Avenue. Denny also operated the Opry Talent Agency, and Hank knew that if he were going to get a spot on the world-famous stage, it would be through this man. Hank immediately found Denny to be friendly and accommodating and supportive of young musicians struggling to find their way in the highly competitive business. The first meeting went well, and without having Hank audition Denny invited him to start at the Opry on January 7, 1950. Hank would be paid seventy dollars a week for the show.

Hank didn't question his good fortune. Performing on the Grand Ole Opry had been his dream for many years. Now he was being offered the chance to be a part of what was considered the world's greatest country music show. This opportunity, Hank felt, would push him to the top of the competitive country music business. At fifty thousand watts, WSM could be heard over most of North America. By performing on the Opry, Hank was about to get national exposure in the U.S. for the first time. But he had a lot to do before he took his place on the famous stage. He had about a month to participate in Denny's publicity push while making arrangements to have his family move to Nashville. It was a whirlwind of activity that required a great deal of juggling, but he managed, and never, for one minute, regretted or second-guessed what he had to do.

Hank, Jimmie, and Minnie in front of their rental house in Nashville.

As part of the advertising blitz to promote Hank Snow as one of the Opry's most promising new stars, Denny helped him get new photographs and prepare a press kit to be sent to radio stations and record buyers. He also purchased ads in the best-known trade papers of the time, such as *Cashbox*, *Billboard*, and *Variety*, exposing Hank to the behind-the-scenes business of country music first-hand. It was a great experience to see someone else promoting him, as in the past that work had mostly fallen to Hank. Within days of arriving in Nashville, he was meeting legendary entertainers, including Eddy Arnold, a singer he had admired for many years, as well as powerful radio DJs, including Hugh Cherry, who, it was said, could make or break a career simply by deciding whether or not to play an artist on his show.

Through Eddy Arnold, Hank met real estate agent Clarence E. Chance, who found Hank a small house to rent on Sarver Avenue in Madison, about ten kilometres from Nashville. The house had plenty of room for the family of three and a good-sized yard for Jimmie and the dogs to play in. The agent also agreed to find a safe and comfortable place for Shawnee while the Snows searched for a permanent home. Jimmie remembers that the rental house was small but provided the family with everything they needed, and they were happy there.

With things moving at a rapid pace, Hank quickly returned to Dallas to share the good news with Minnie and Jimmie. They packed up and headed to Nashville to start a new chapter in the life of Hank Snow, country music singer, songwriter, and showman. At thirty-five, he had overcome many odds and come all the way from Brooklyn, Nova Scotia, to the greatest stage of all: the Grand Ole Opry.

Once in Nashville, the Snows quickly settled into their new surroundings. Hank always said he immediately felt at home there. To fill the time while awaiting his Opry debut and in an effort to meet new people, Hank did a few shows around town, but he felt he was more than ready for the big time. Backed by Tubb's band, the Texas Troubadours, Hank Snow made his first Grand Ole Opry appearance on January 7, 1950. He took the legendary stage where so many country music stars had performed following these words from his friend, Ernest Tubb: "From up Canada way, here's the newest member of the Grand Ole Opry: The Singing Ranger, Hank Snow."

For his first performance, Hank sang "Brand on My Heart," and despite a lukewarm reception from the audience that almost prompted him to quit, he went back to the Opry and gave it his all. As Minnie pointed out to him following that first performance, Hank had come too far, worked too hard, and had made too many sacrifices to give up just as he was on the brink of achieving his dreams. He had to give the audience a chance to discover him, she suggested. He was good, she told him, and she would not hear of him quitting. It was an opportunity of a lifetime and if he walked away at that point, he would never get a second chance. Besides, she pointed out, what else would he do?

Minnie's words resonated with Hank. Hoping she was right, Hank decided that the only way to ensure his place at the Opry was to be the best performer he could be. If not for Minnie, he often said, he might have quit and left Nashville after that night, but she had stuck with him through difficult times in the past and always offered sound advice so he listened when she spoke. Making country music on records and on the radio was all he had been dreaming of for years, and he was just about there. This was not the time to give up, she told him. With that ultimate goal in mind, Hank became more determined than ever. He hired his own band, starting with steel guitar player Joe Talbot and fiddle player Tommy Vader. Together, they created the legendary sound that would soon become synonymous with Hank Snow's music.

Memories of those early days in Nashville have remained with Jimmie Rodgers Snow his entire life and, he says, they are mostly good ones. "It was a whole new world for Mother and I when we finally moved to Nashville, Tennessee, in 1949," he remembers.

> I sure do remember those nights going to the Grand Ole Opry with my Dad, and sitting on the wings of the stage close to the announcer's booth, watching all those great stars that I used to listen to on the radio in Nova Scotia. How exciting—Red Foley, Hank Williams, Ernie Ford, Kay Star, and so many more that I never dreamed I would ever see. I was privileged to enjoy every Friday and Saturday night on the stage of the Opry.

A few weeks after Hank's Opry debut, Steve Sholes came to Nashville to record several of the RCA Victor artists, among them Hank Snow, providing he had some original material to record. He did. And he knew the only way to get the reception he wanted and to guarantee his continuation at the Opry was to have a hit record. Although Sholes had previously rejected "I'm Movin' On" during Hank's earlier recording session in Chicago, Hank was confident this song was the answer. He vowed that he wouldn't let Sholes reject it. With his friends Tommy and Joe as backup, Hank was determined to record the song this time. He knew it was good and he just had a feeling about the song.

At 7:00 P.M. on March 28, 1950, Hank and his band gathered for a recording session at a place in downtown Nashville known as Brown's Studio. With the opening notes of the song's trademark fiddle and steel guitar riffs, Hank recorded what would become the most important song of his career, a song which he once said took him about fifteen minutes to write—the first draft at least—but carried him to places he couldn't even dream of. Along with "I'm Movin' On" he also recorded "With This

Hank Snow, an RCA Victor hitmaker.

Ring I Thee Wed," "Paving the Highway With Tears," and "I Cried But My Tears Were Too Late."

While he felt his first Nashville recording session had gone well, Hank continued to struggle for acceptance at the Opry where he was still getting lukewarm audience reception. He believed his stay at the famous venue was tenuous at best. As he waited for his first release from that session, he continued to perform there with only moderate success, and he was quickly becoming disillusioned. He feared that if he didn't soon have a major hit, his time at the Opry could be limited. He would later learn that his fear had been dangerously close to becoming realized.

Just when Hank was beginning to think he would never have a major hit in the U.S., "I'm Movin' On" was released by RCA. No sooner had the record hit the airwaves in April 1950 than it began to race up the country music charts with a velocity befitting its name, one which had rarely been seen before in the history of the country music charts. The hit came just at the right time—Hank's time at the Opry had just about run out. However, all that changed with the massive hit record.

"After that hit song, Dad's career took off faster than we would have ever thought, bringing about tremendous changes," says Jimmie, reflecting on that period in his father's life. "Our lifestyle was one of these changes. We had gone from being extremely poor to suddenly becoming rich, exchanging the small house for the large house. Both homes are still there today, and are reminders of these early years.

Postcard featuring Hank Snow, The Singing Ranger, star of the WSM Grand Ole Opry.

Being part of the early Nashville scene, which was huge then but is a much larger industry today, was exciting."

Up to that point, the charts hadn't seen a song move so quickly or carry as much momentum. "I'm Movin' On" was destined to make history. Quickly becoming Hank's signature song, the record held the number one position on the country music charts for an unprecedented twenty-nine weeks and stayed on the charts for an incredible fourteen months. According to some modern record books, "I'm Movin' On" holds the distinction of being the most-played country music song of all time. Equally impressive was the fact that not only was the song a massive hit, but the flip side of the record, "With This Ring I Thee Wed," also became a huge success for Hank. And there was more to come—much more.

Not bad for a poor boy from the South Shore of Nova Scotia who spent much of his youth not knowing where his next meal was going to come from, or where he was going to sleep at night. In the wake of his impressive record, Hank Snow's dreams were becoming a reality.

On the Road

After being raised in poverty and struggling to survive through the most challenging circumstances, after all the sacrifices he and his family made over the years, and after chasing his dreams across the continent, Hank Snow had finally arrived. He had paid his dues and now, not only was he playing at the Grand Ole Opry, but he had scored a monster radio hit and his music was being heard by millions of people.

Through sheer determination and hard work, Hank had reached his destination. To reward himself, he purchased a home in the Nashville suburb of Madison. The modest bungalow was the first and only house the Snows ever owned. It sat on a one-hectare (three-acre) lot on which Hank had a barn built for Shawnee. As soon as they moved in, Hank began to refer to the place as Rainbow Ranch. He also took to calling his band The Rainbow Ranch Boys in honour of his home, and the name stuck.

With the hit records and regular work at the Opry, Hank could have afforded to hire a maid to help Minnie care for the house, but she preferred to do the work herself (which she did right up until her advancing age made it too difficult). However, Hank did hire a handyman to help around the property. Willie Fred Carter, better known as "Squirlie," did a variety of jobs, including the gardening, running errands, doing repairs, and taking care of Shawnee and the two dogs that had been the family's companions for several years.

As a member of the Grand Ole Opry, Hank was now being sent out on tour with other Opry stars, including his new friend Hank Williams. For each tour, Hank was paid five hundred dollars. Compared to his previous rate of pay, which, if he were lucky, would have been around twenty-five dollars a day, Hank was now in the elite echelon of the country music business, and it felt good.

Minnie at Rainbow Ranch, 1958.

With the success of "I'm Movin' On" and the song's staying power on the charts, Hank continued to tour while his career built momentum, criss-crossing Canada and the United States. In the coming years, Hank would see much of North America and a great deal of the world as the appeal of country music spread around the globe.

By 1951, Hank Snow had become a major country music star, and even though he was now doing what he had dreamed of doing since his childhood days back in Nova Scotia, it wasn't all a bed of roses. In his autobiography, he writes: "The pressure of the hectic life I was living sometimes got to me. Being on the road so much, rushing around from plane to plane, dealing with problems, trying to be pleasant when you didn't feel well, playing in hot, stuffy halls where there was no air-conditioning would zap your energy real fast and make you less than cheerful."

During this era, whenever an artist was on the road but close to Nashville, he or she was required by contract to return to the Opry for the Saturday night show, which was broadcast coast to coast. Hank always met his obligation, and understood its necessity, but having to travel even more to get back to Nashville added to the stress of life

Jimmie and Hank with The Rainbow Ranch Boys at Hank's home record-ing studio.

on the road. Hank occasionally turned to alcohol for relief from the great pressure, a move that sometimes got him into trouble and was something he would regret later in life.

Recognizing his own tendency, and that of others in the indus-try, to stray to the bottle, Hank established several policies for himself and members of his band. For starters, it was understood that none of them would drink alcohol before a show. Hank was so adamant about that policy that he would not hire anyone who would not agree to that stipulation. As well, if any band member had been drinking the night before a show and was not likely to meet Hank's standards on stage, then he was not permitted to perform. Band member Kayton Roberts recalls that while he travelled many roads and did many shows with Hank, he couldn't remember seeing Hank drinking before going on stage. "We had a good time together, and Hank was good to the band members, but he was very strict with that policy," he says.

Hank was strict about his rules, but he also admitted that there were times he broke the one he had about drinking before going on stage. It was a Sunday following his Opry performance. He was sched-uled to do two shows that day in Gulfport, Mississippi, but the travel and lack of sleep was too stressful for him, and he drank a little too much vodka to relax and ease the tension. Although he played the shows, he didn't feel he was really in any shape to stand in front of an audience. He insisted, though, that this was one of the few times he ever went on stage after drinking, and he regretted that he had set a bad example for his band members.

Eventually, Hank chose to quit drinking altogether. He had his last taste of alcohol on March 31, 1970, and he said he was the better for quitting. He gave up smoking, his other bad habit, in 1979 following a medical checkup. While he was still in good health at the time, he resolved that as he was getting older he should take better care of himself and giving up cigarettes was one thing he could control.

As the 1950s wore on amid the shadow of the Korean War, which broke out in June 1950, Hank enjoyed a steady climb up the ladder of fame, becoming one of the most successful and recognizable country music artists of his era. With number-one hits on the radio, record-breaking sales, regular shows at the Opry, and tours that kept him on the road most of the year, personal appearances by Hank Snow were in high demand. Despite his busy schedule, however, in March 1953 he managed to find the time to travel to Korea to entertain the American troops stationed there, a cause that was important to him. Fourteen Opry stars, including Hank Snow and his Rainbow Ranch Boys and Ernest Tubb and the Texas Troubadors, volunteered their time and talents to go to Korea for three weeks and Japan for another week.

Hank estimated the Opry stars entertained thousands of troops in Korea, and he rated it as one of the most rewarding and personally fulfilling experiences of his music career. While he had never been to war, Hank felt that he could do his part by boosting the morale of those brave soldiers who were fighting for their country thousands of kilometres from home.

In his book, Hank writes:

> We were flown to a number of places and we entertained one group after another. We played to several hundred troops on a makeshift stage and, as you would expect, the GIs loved hearing country music from home. During our shows and at night we often heard gunfire and

mortar fire in the background. It was a dangerous and dismal atmosphere and I had sympathy for the poor boys who were sacrificing so much for their country.

One of the most popular requests Hank received during his Korean tour was for "My Mother," the hit song he had written years earlier in honour of his own mother and which he had first recorded on the RCA Victor Bluebird label in 1945. Understanding that the soldiers, many of them still very young, were stationed far from home in a foreign land, he was moved to do something special for them. He announced after he performed the song at each show that if the men would give him their mothers' names and addresses, he would in turn personally write to each of their mothers when he returned to the United States to say that he had seen their sons and that they were doing fine.

Thinking he might receive only a few hundred requests, he was overwhelmed when he received more than seven thousand names and addresses from the servicemen. However, true to his word, when he returned to Nashville, Hank hired a secretary to address the envelopes and had a form letter printed. Then he personally signed each, "With love, Hank Snow." He did all of this at his own expense. Hank felt it was the least he could do for the soldiers and their mothers.

The Ups and Downs of Fame

As Hank's fame grew, his pace also intensified. Not only did he travel to Korea and tour nonstop to promote his records, but he and Ernest Tubb also undertook a major project, largely at their own expense, to establish a permanent memorial in Meridian, Mississippi, the home of Jimmie Rodgers. Also known as "the Singing Brakeman" and "the Blue Yodeler," Rodgers is largely considered by most historians to be the Father of Country Music, and both Hank and Tubb credited Rodgers as a major influence in their own music careers.

Jimmie Rodgers Snow, named after the legendary singer, recalls his father often saying that he pursued country music largely because of the inspiration he drew from the early recording artist. Rodgers's music was especially important to Hank during those difficult years when he was struggling to make a living and may have been questioning his choices. Somehow, Jimmie says, his father found the courage and inspiration through Rodgers's music to keep pushing forward, and he believed it was that sense of gratitude that led to his father's desire to give something back to the man from whom he had drawn so much.

The Jimmie Rodgers Memorial Festival in Meridian is held every May to honour the anniversary of Rodgers's death. The first festival, on May 26, 1953, included the unveiling of a major statue, which was created largely through the efforts of Hank and Tubb. The memorial stands today in the town's park, and Hank considered the project to have been one of his major accomplishments, as it allowed him to pay homage to the man who he mostly credited for his interest in country music.

By 1953 Hank's career was definitely on a roll. But despite all his success, his world came crashing down when he received word from back home in Liverpool that his mother had taken ill following

The grand street attracted thousands of spectators to Meridian, Mississippi, each year to participate in the Jimmie Rodgers Memorial Festival. Leading one of the early parades were (left to right) Hank Snow, Jimmie Rodgers's wife, Carrie, and Ernest Tubb.

two serious strokes that had affected her mental and physical capacities. He was devastated by the news. Although by this time Hank was now fully established in Nashville, he had maintained contact with his family, staying in touch with his sisters who still lived in his hometown. This allowed him to track his mother's status. By September, doctors were advising Hank to come home if he wanted to see her one last time. So with heavy hearts, the family drove to Liverpool for what would be Hank's final visit with his beloved mother.

With commitments back in Nashville, Hank could only stay in Liverpool a few days, but he cherished the time he had with his ailing

Standing in front of the Jimmie Rodgers Memorial are, from left, Hank Snow, Ernest Tubb, Jimmie Rodgers Snow, and Carrie Rodgers.

mother who, by then, had grown weak and thin. While it was difficult to leave her, Hank took fond memories with him when he returned to Nashville. "I didn't say goodbye," he writes in his book. "I couldn't."

In Nashville, it was hard getting back into a business routine as Hank waited for the dreaded news from his hometown, but he had commitments, including a twenty-one-day tour that would take him throughout the Pacific Northwest and into British Columbia. In light of his mother's tenuous condition, he didn't feel he should go on tour, but he felt he had no other option, and he also felt his mother would tell him to honour his commitments. As he tried to carry on, Hank maintained constant contact with his family in Liverpool, receiving regular updates wherever he travelled. Hank's mother succumbed to her illness at the age of sixty-four on October 18, 1953, while Hank was en route by plane to Vancouver. He learned of her death when he reached his destination.

The loss of his mother was devastating for Hank, and although he wanted to immediately fly back to Liverpool to attend her funeral, it wasn't possible. Instead, although it was difficult but because he believed his mother would tell him to, Hank decided to carry on with his concerts. He did his show the next day as a tribute to her, and always said that going on the stage that night was the most difficult thing he ever had to do in all of his years in show business. He closed the show with his song, "My Mother" and the appreciative audience responded warmly with what he believed was of one of the longest standing ovations of his career.

Thirteen years following Hank's mother's death, while he was on tour again, Hank's father became seriously ill. Snow senior died in 1966 at age eighty. Again, under contract, Hank managed to carry through with his shows, closing his performances with the song, "That Silver-Haired Daddy of Mine" in his father's honour.

By the mid-1950s, Hank had established himself as one of the premier country music artists in the industry, chalking up an impressive list of number one hits, headlining successful concert tours, and pulling large crowds into the Grand Ole Opry. Hits such as "I'm Movin' On" and its follow-up smash "The Golden Rocket" were making music-chart history. Riding on Hank's success, RCA Victor continued to release his records, which continued to rule the charts for much of the decade and into the better part of the next. Hank often referred to that era as his "golden period," taking great pride in what he had achieved. Few other artists from that time could boast equal success, and the fact that Hank had fought and clawed his way from obscurity in a small village on the rocky shores of Nova Scotia to international fame and acclaim not only allowed him to appreciate his achievements but also made his story more compelling.

During this time, RCA released a string of Hank Snow songs that dominated the charts, many of them reaching and holding the number one position, establishing records for their longevity and lasting power. Many of those records stand today and a number of their hits, such as "I'm Movin,' On," "I Don't Hurt Anymore," "The Rhumba Boogie," "The Golden Rocket," "I've Been Everywhere," "Let Me Go, Lover," and "Hello Love," are considered country music standards, often emulated by contemporary artists who credit Hank Snow among their influences.

Also during this time, Hank toured extensively, performing in front of crowds in the thousands, a far cry from the shows he had played throughout the 1940s. In addition to the hit records and large audiences, Hank began winning awards, both from within the country music industry and from fans. One of his first major accolades came in 1951 when readers of *Southern Farmer* magazine voted him America's favourite country and folk singer, even though Hank was a Canadian citizen. It was among the first of many awards he won over the years for his singing and songwriting. Hank was particularly pleased by any recognition he received for songwriting. He was once quoted as saying that it was difficult to put into words how he found the skills to write songs, but in his book, he writes, "You can't just snap your fingers and jump into the mood you want. No matter where or how the song comes to you, I do know that all the ingredients have to be just right in order to have a hit song."

While he was an accomplished and well-regarded songwriter in his own right, Hank wasn't opposed to recording songs written by others, many of which went on to become huge Hank Snow hits; most notable of those were compositions such as "(Now And Then There's) A Fool Such As I," written by Bill Trader and recorded by Hank in 1952; "I Don't Hurt Anymore," written by Don Robertson and Jack

Hank Snow and The Rainbow Ranch Boys in the mid-1950s.

Rollins, and recorded by Hank in 1954; and "I've Been Everywhere," written by Geoff Mack and recorded by Hank in 1962.

The bottom line, Hank said, was that when it came to recording, it really didn't matter who wrote the song, just as long as it was good and the singer knew what to do with it. Hank was extremely particular about the songs he sang. He knew exactly what he liked and which songs would best suit his vocal style, and he wouldn't let anyone talk him into recording a song he didn't believe in. This commitment to his "sound" caused Snow to pass up the opportunity to record two songs that Hank Williams had written for him before he died on January 1, 1953. One of those songs was the country classic "Jambalaya," and the other was a tune called "You Better Keep It On Your Mind," both of which went on to become huge hits for Williams.

While he said he passed on those songs because he didn't think they suited his style, Snow often admitted regretting that he had not found the perfect Williams song to record while his friend was still alive, but when it didn't feel right, Snow had to trust his gut. However, he did eventually record a Williams's composition called "Mansion On the Hill" as a tribute to the legendary singer-songwriter.

Throughout his life, Hank was always quick to recognize those who had helped him along his way, including entertainers such as Ernest Tubb, Hank Williams, Eddy Arnold, Hawkshaw Hawkins, and Marty Robbins, with whom he became very close friends after arriving in Nashville. He also credited many industry insiders, songwriters, musicians, managers, and promoters for much of his success. He could also pinpoint the people who were less than helpful, and the one person he detested more than anyone else was Colonel Tom Parker, the man largely credited with "discovering" and managing Elvis Presley, King of Rock and Roll. But there is more to the Elvis Presley story than most people know.

At one time, Snow and Parker—Hank refused to call him Colonel—were business partners in a deal to manage Presley. It was a deal in which Hank insisted he was "robbed," and that turned the two into bitter enemies. Hank so despised Parker that he held the grudge against him until he died. The feud started in 1954, when Hank was looking for a new agent to oversee his personal appearances, media interviews, and contract negotiations. Hank met with Parker to arrange a deal—one he eventually said he regretted. He had to live with the decision that he called a major mistake for the rest of his life.

Hank's initial impression of Parker, who had offices in a back corner of a small garage next to a modest home in a neighbourhood not far from Hank's own place, was not encouraging, but he shrugged it off. Again, Hank said, he should have gone with his gut. Parker not only became his manager by 1954, but the two subsequently became business partners, forming a company known as Hank Snow Enterprises–Jamboree Attractions. The company was a fifty-fifty partnership that combined the assets of both men. Under the auspices of this company, Hank toured as the headline attraction with a list of supporting entertainers as opening acts, including Jimmie Rodgers Snow and an energetic up-and-comer named Elvis Presley, who came on the scene in early 1955.

In fact, Jimmie recalls, when his father first heard of Elvis Presley, the young man was still relatively unknown in the entertainment world. Although Hank acknowledged that he learned about this raw, young talent from Memphis, Tennessee, through Parker, it was actually Hank who arranged to have him appear on the Grand Ole Opry during one of his own appearances, and it was Hank who introduced Presley to the famous stage for the first time in January 1958. Elvis sang one of his early hits, "Blue Moon of Kentucky," during that debut performance, his one and only appearance ever on the

Jimmie and Hank Snow at one of the shows put on by Hank Snow Enterprises–Jamboree Attractions.

Opry. Hank described Elvis as "one of the finest and most polite gentlemen I had ever known," one who "soon became a very close friend to my family and me."

In particular, Elvis became very close to Hank's son, Jimmie, who was also pursuing his own country music career at that time with an RCA record deal. Elvis spent a lot of time at the Snow home in those early years, and Jimmie enjoyed the company of the talented young man very much.

As a seventeen-year-old teenager I became a part of the show business world travelling to show dates with my Dad and having a career of my own, recording singles on the RCA Victor label, working shows with the greats of the day, like Elvis Presley, Andy Griffith, Jim Reeves, Johnny Cash and many more—all these wonderful stars being part of this scene. There was a time that Elvis was around our home so much that we considered him to be a member of the family. We were all very close friends and Dad always had great fondness

A young Jimmie Rodgers Snow was making a name for himself with his own RCA record contract and opening for his father's concerts.

for Elvis, even after things fell part with Parker. Dad recognized the raw talent right away and was happy to do anything he could to help Elvis.

As 1955 unfolded, Hank and Parker continued to put on shows, sometimes using as the major attraction other entertainers like Andy Griffith, who went on to become a major television star, and other times using Hank as the headliner. They used young talent like Jimmie and Elvis, who were usually paid $250 a week, to open the shows. But

Hank recognized something special in this young man from Memphis, and he knew early on that Elvis was destined to have a huge career.

Upon witnessing the audience's reaction to Elvis during these shows, Hank eventually asked Elvis to switch places with him in the lineup. When it became clear to Hank that Elvis would work the audience into a frenzy with his high-energy brand of music, he felt it was more fitting to close the show on that note than with Hank's more mellow style. "This was unheard of back then, as the headline was supposed to be the major attraction, but it was actually Dad's idea to move things around," Jimmie says. "Dad was the one who went to Elvis with the plan because he felt it would be better for the show and Dad was all about doing what was best for the show. His idea was to always give the audience what they wanted."

It was clear that Hank had a lot of influence over Elvis. It was also Hank who talked Elvis into signing with the agency owned by Hank Snow and Tom Parker, telling him it was important to have proper guidance as his career took off. And it was also largely through Hank's efforts and contacts that RCA finally signed Elvis to a record deal.

Hank's association with Parker lasted only about a year and a half, but it was one of the most tumultuous times in Hank's life. In the end, the partnership dissolved under a cloud of discontent and controversy. Hank was surprised to learn that Parker had not, in fact, signed Elvis Presley to Hank Snow Enterprises–Jamboree Attractions as they had agreed, but instead, by using two contracts and sleight of hand, Colonel Tom Parker had tricked Elvis and his parents into signing an exclusive arrangement with him. According to the terms of that document, Hank had no claim on the young talent he had helped to develop. "Dad took that whole thing

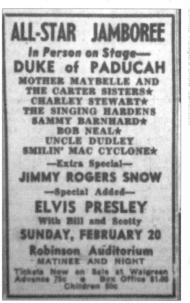

This newspaper ad from 1954 or 1955 shows the scheduled lineup. Note Elvis's name is closer to the bottom, as he was still relatively unknown.

very hard," Jimmie recalls. "He couldn't believe that anyone would do something like that and he never forgave Parker what he had done."

The years that followed were tough for Hank, Jimmie says, as his father watched Elvis shoot to international stardom and achieve a level of success unequalled in the music business. Make no mistake, Jimmie stresses, Hank was happy for the young man's success, but felt that Parker had cheated him out of being part of that success. And it wasn't all about the money, Jimmie says. It was also about receiving credit for helping to develop such an incredible talent that continues to resonate with the world even after all this time. While Jimmie says that Hank thought about suing Parker on many occasions, his father's lawyers advised against it, as they thought the battle would be long, dirty, and costly.

In the end, the lawyers also thought Hank would lose the legal battle, since Parker had the exclusive contract signed by Elvis. Regardless of how Parker had gotten the signature, the bottom line was that he had it, and everything else was a matter of Hank's word against Parker's. But, Jimmie says, his father never could get over the feeling that he had been tricked and cheated out of something major, and he despised Parker for the deceit. "He could never forgive him," Jimmie says.

Regardless of what had transpired between himself and Parker, however, Hank maintained great respect for Elvis, remembering him as a fine young man and a great talent, unlike anyone before him or since. It was a sad day for Hank when Elvis died, Jimmie says, for so many reasons. In a lot of ways it was like Hank had lost a member of his own family. Not only was it a major loss to the entertainment world, but Hank was disheartened by the erroneous information that was published about their relationship and of his own involvement with Parker. Despite many requests, Hank never spoke publicly about the contract dispute until he wrote about it in his book. When he did so, he felt he had finally set the record straight.

Hank summed it up succinctly for me when I interviewed him in 1991: "Me and Tom Parker—Presley's long-time manager—operated a talent agency in the 1950s and we discovered him. Parker stole my part of Presley, but I don't like to talk too much about that."

THE GOLDEN YEARS

When Opportunity Knocks

In addition to making records and touring to support his music, Hank Snow also developed a reputation as an astute businessman. During the 1950s and 1960s, he kept his eyes open for potential investment opportunities. Hank, along with Ernest Tubb, invested in two radio stations, one in Whitesburg, Kentucky, and the other in Harriman, Tennessee. The partners bought the stations in 1954 and sold them three years later at a good profit. It seemed like a prudent move, Hank often joked, considering he and Ernest really didn't know what they were doing.

Another unique business opportunity came along in 1958, when Hank purchased a music store located on Nashville's Church Street along with a forty-one-foot cabin cruiser, which he named *The Golden Rocket*. Following an extensive renovation of the building, The Hank Snow Music Center Inc. and School of Music was opened amid much fanfare. Here, students were taught to read music and play a variety of instruments, such as the guitar and fiddle. It was a proud time for Hank, who believed he had made a sound business investment. In addition to the store and school, he also formed the Silver Star Music Company and the East Star Music Company, both of which had offices in the same building.

Although Hank admitted that the profit from The Hank Snow Music Center Inc. and School of Music wasn't great, he pointed out that the business served other purposes. Every Friday evening, for example, the store hosted a live radio show that was broadcast over the WSM

Hank Snow Music Center, August 1962.

radio station, which reached approximately thirty-five stations across the U.S. and provided great publicity for him, ultimately leading to more customers. After nine years in the music store, however, Hank sold the business, as it became too much for him to handle along with his successful singing career, which was still keeping him on the road for much of the year.

Sheri Blackwood was Hank's personal assistant for over twenty-seven years. She recalls that her association with Hank actually started somewhere around 1968, when she went to work for him at his publishing company. "I had classes in the morning and landed a part-time job at Silver Star Music in West Nashville, which Hank owned. I worked from 1 P.M. to 5 P.M., and Hank signed all my cheques but I never saw him. Troy Martin ran the office, but Hank had a private office there and only came in at night."

Sheri viewed Hank as an astute businessman who chose his business partners carefully.

> Troy was well known in the music business—a very successful publisher back to his days working with Gene Autry's music company. With Hank and Troy running the company, there was a steady flow of songwriters plugging their songs and artists looking for a hit to record. I could tell by the way they glanced at the closed office door, they were wondering if Hank was in there... he wasn't. I remember when Opry members Carl and Pearl Butler were there one afternoon, and Pearl was talking to me while Carl listened to songs. She asked me if Hank was as private a person as everyone said he

was. She laughed when I told her I didn't know—that I'd worked for him four months and I'd never met him.

Thinking back on that time, Sheri says she isn't sure how long it was after that that she finally did meet Hank. Her job at the ranch actually came about after Hank's publishing company became embroiled in a lawsuit and closed down.

The company had a huge hit by Billy Walker called "A Million and One." It had been covered by a lot of major artists and was well over a million in sales. Another publishing company, Acuff-Rose, brought a lawsuit saying the company had infringed on their song, "I Can't Stop Loving You." Hank was busy on the road with his own career at this time and didn't feel our small company could afford to go up against a powerhouse like Acuff-Rose. He gave them the publishing rights and closed the company...a big mistake, which he later came to regret.

That's what brought about Sheri's actual move from his publishing company to his private office at Rainbow Ranch. "He asked me to work there and finalize the transfer of our song catalog to his other music companies, operated by Hill & Range in New York. At that point, I guess I thought I didn't need to be going to school anymore, so I started working full-time for him from 9 to 5. When the catalog transfer was completed, there was never any discussion of me leaving."

And, she adds, she never had any regrets about staying.

Throughout the 1950s and 1960s, Hank Snow was hitting the height of his success, releasing one hit record after the other and touring extensively, criss-crossing North America and performing widely throughout Europe, including stops at many American military bases and entertaining for the GIs stationed overseas, something Hank took great pride in doing. Usually the band played two shows a night on these bases, one for the enlisted men and a second for the noncommissioned offices. No matter how many shows they did on these bases, Hank always considered it an honour to play for the soldiers and he was happy to bring them a little piece of home.

The regular cast members of the Grand Ole Opry from 1963. Hank Snow is sixth from the left in the bottom row.

A highlight of the European tours for Hank was a show he did in 1972 at the London Palladium, after which he received a surprise backstage visit from Ringo Starr. As it turned out, Ringo was a huge fan of Hank Snow and of country music in general. It was a thrill for Hank to meet another artist who appreciated what he did, and he felt it was proof of the power of country music to build many bridges.

Sheri recalls, "Hank had this undeniable greatness that was acclaimed by some of the biggest names in the business: Bob Dylan, Elvis Presley, Merle Haggard, Johnny Cash, The Rolling Stones, and so many others. It was especially exciting for me when Hank called the office one day during an early '70s tour of England and said, 'Oh by the way, Ringo Starr came to see my show last night...' He was thrilled."

In fact, in 1970, Ringo was the first Beatle to record an album in the United States, choosing Nashville as the place to record, cutting songs by Nashville writers and backed by Nashville musicians. He was such a country music fan that one writer, Peter Cooper, noted in a July 12, 2012, blog titled Happy Birthday Ringo Starr that "His Rolls Royce is equipped with a cartridge player which plays tapes by Ernest Tubb, Hank Snow and other country artists."

Hank Snow meets Ringo Starr backstage in 1972.

Travel to foreign lands became part of the routine for Hank and his Rainbow Ranch Boys. His increased popularity on the music charts led to concert tours of exotic places and faraway countries like Japan, places Hank could only dream about as a boy growing up in rural Nova Scotia. And as Jimmie says, "Having the chance to travel with Dad on some of these trips was a real learning experience for me. It's true that travelling can be tough on some young people, but for me, this was better than any education I could have received in school, because I had the opportunity to see the world and experience all kinds of things first-hand. What better education is there than actually living the experience?"

One of Hank's most memorable trips was when he and The Rainbow Ranch Boys, along with Jimmie Rodgers Snow and his wife, Carolee Cooper, spent the Christmas of 1966 in Vietnam entertaining the troops stationed there. Just as during the Korean War, Hank felt that entertaining the troops was one way he could make a contribution to the effort. If his music brought some comfort to the men and women who were thousands of kilometres away from home in a war zone, then he was prepared to do whatever he could to give them a

During their tour of Vietman in December 1966, the performers received an award for their service from Donald H. McGovern, Brigadier General of the U.S. military. To the left of Hank are The Rainbow Ranch Boys. To the right are Jimmie's wife, Carolee Cooper, Jimmie Rodgers Snow, and the group's escort officer.

reprieve, if only for a short while. He felt his personal sacrifice for a few weeks paled in comparison to that being made by the GIs.

Jimmie recalls that particular tour was one of the most memorable excursions he made with his father. "Performing in a war zone, as you can imagine, came with its own challenges, but this was something Dad felt we had to do for the troops," he says. "And we were happy to do our part to support the effort, despite the dangers."

As Jimmie points out, for an entertainer such as Hank Snow, touring to support his music was a top priority, as reaching his fans was important to him, but it was more than that to his father. "He truly enjoyed connecting with his audience and playing his music for them," he says. "The fans were very important to him because they are the ones who made it all happen."

Long-time band member Kayton Roberts echoes that sentiment. "Hank was great with his fans," he recalls.

> They were very important to him. He was especially warm and friendly with people who had disabilities. I had

seen him on many occasions go out into the audience and shake the hand of someone in a wheelchair. He'd stop and talk to them sometimes in between songs and hold up the set. He was really good with people who came to see him. He'd say, "They paid good money to come and watch me sing and I've got to show them the respect they deserve." I think that says something important about Hank's character and the kind of man he was.

Changing Times

As country music became more pop oriented throughout the 1970s and 1980s, traditional country artists like Hank Snow found it difficult to adapt to the changing tastes. In turn, country music radio started pushing the older, more traditional, performers to the background in favour of more contemporary, so-called "cross-over" artists, who were selling large volumes of records.

Finally, in 1981, after a forty-five-year relationship with RCA/ RCA Victor—the longest any artist has ever been on one label—Hank Snow and the record company that had given him his start more than four and a half decades earlier in Montreal parted ways. The label had decided to pare down its roster by eliminating artists considered no longer relevant in the modern market.

Jimmie Rodgers Snow recalls that this was a difficult time for his father. Hank had hoped the executives making the decisions at that time would keep him around long enough to at least mark his fiftieth anniversary with the label. Jimmie agrees that for RCA, the chance to put together a collection of music spanning fifty years of hits on one label would have been an amazing project, but they weren't interested. Instead, they dropped Hank Snow simply because he wasn't considered contemporary, despite the fact that he still had legions of fans around the world and was still selling millions of records. "When they let him go, they missed an excellent opportunity to sell a lot of records," Jimmie says. "How many artists reach that milestone?"

Those around Hank recognized that the breakup with RCA was extremely hard on him and was a turning point in his illustrious career, signalling that things were beginning to wind down for the legendary singer. Several other record companies approached Hank after the split with RCA. He never took any of the offers, but in 1985 he was lured back into the studio for one more project: he recorded an album with Willie Nelson called *Brand On My Heart* for Columbia Records. Sheri Blackwood, Hank's long-time personal assistant, recalls that Hank was extremely proud of it. "He said it was one of the best he had ever done," she says.

When I interviewed Hank in 1991 and asked how he felt modern country music differed from the earlier brand of music that was being played when he started, he hesitated, then said, "I don't really believe things are that much different now than they were back then. The country music industry in Canada is growing a little, but if you want to have major success, I still believe you have to come to the United States where the market is. Country music has been good for me and I've seen many changes in my time, but I don't have any regrets about spending my life in the business."

After fifty-five years on the road, although not fully retired, Hank had pulled back on touring by the mid-1980s and made only the occasional personal appearance, including a few visits to his native, Nova Scotia, and his birthplace, Brooklyn, Queens County. His last excursion to the Maritimes was in the summer of 1982, when Irving Oil Limited sponsored a "coming home" party for Hank Snow. Called Irving Oil Country Days, the tour, which was part of Nova Scotia's Old Home Summer promotion, included five concerts throughout Nova Scotia—Kentville, Dartmouth, Bridgewater, Truro, and Sydney—as well as a stop in Brooklyn, and a major celebration dinner in Halifax hosted by then Nova Scotia premier John Buchanan and attended by several hundred guests.

During that homecoming tour, Hank remained somewhat secluded and sheltered from the press and general public, seeing only close personal friends and family, but he did make one public appearance other than the concerts and dinner. On the afternoon of July 15, he returned to Brooklyn to celebrate the opening of a children's playground that had been constructed on the site where his family homestead had previously stood. During that hot summer afternoon, Hank held any painful memories he may have harboured in check. He talked to the crowd of well-wishers, shook hands, signed autographs, and reconnected with long-lost acquaintances as they reminisced about growing up in the small, Depression-era village.

"I remember him when he used to play for parties and family get-togethers around here," one local resident was quoted in a July 21, 1982, article in *The Advance*, Queens County's community newspaper. Most people gathered at the site that day agreed that it was hard to comprehend how a man from this small village on the southern coast of Nova Scotia could overcome so much adversity and thrive.

Hank was overwhelmed with the warm welcome he received in his hometown and was particularly impressed that the

Invitation for Irving Oil Country Days, starring Hank Snow and Carroll Baker.

(now shuttered) Bowater Mersey Paper Company had taken the land that the company had obtained in 1979 and donated it to the Village of Brooklyn for the purpose of a children's playground, a fitting use for the property considering its history. More than anything, Hank was humbled that the company and the village commissioners had chosen to build the playground in his honour.

"I'll never forget Brooklyn and the people who live here, because it's my home and it's where it all began," he said, in addressing the crowd that had gathered that day to see him. "Returning here has brought back some happy memories and some sad memories, but it's sure nice to return...it's hard to describe how it feels to return after so many years." He added that he remembered those early days very well. "How can you forget those days of starving in the streets and not knowing where your next penny will come from?"

However, Hank quickly pointed out to the crowd of fans and friends from his earlier life that no matter where he roamed in the world and despite not returning for such a long time, he never forgot his native Nova Scotian home; many of his song lyrics contain references to his home province, a testament to his love for it. "It has influenced my music in such a way that it's difficult to describe. As a matter of fact, everything in my life has influenced my music."

Although Hank Snow had officially become an American citizen on January 27, 1957, he told those gathered in Brooklyn that day that he still considered himself to be Canadian at heart and in spirit. "Like I always say," he quipped amid the applause, "you can take the boy out of Canada, but you can't take Canada out of the boy." He went on to describe the playground tribute as "one of the greatest honours of my career."

Hank continued to tour every year until 1985, when he finally decided it was time to leave the gruelling demands of the road and devote more time to Minnie, the woman who had always been very supportive of him no matter what he wanted to try or where his dreams led him. As they were both getting older, Hank felt he owed her his time, and with his retirement they spent their senior years together at their home, Rainbow Ranch.

Plaque commemorating the Hank Snow Playground in Brooklyn, Nova Scotia, where Snow was born.

While Hank did continue to make the occasional personal appearance, his last official road date prior to retiring from touring was August 30, 1986, where he first broke onto the American stage: Wheeling, West Virginia. Held every year from July to December, Jamboree USA is a large country music festival held in Wheeling and is the second-oldest country music program in the United States (next to the Grand Ole Opry). Fittingly, Hank shared the bill with fellow country music legend Little Jimmy Dickens, with whom he had become close friends over the years.

Following his retirement from touring, Hank did continue to perform his regular shows at the Opry for roughly another ten years. Officially, the world-famous Grand Ole Opry (of which Hank was a member) is held every Saturday, and Hank made his last appearance on that show on August 31, 1996. He came back the following Friday for the Friday Night Opry on September 6, 1996, his last appearance on the stage. "I Almost Lost My Mind" was the last song he performed there.

One source said of Hank's retirement:

> I remember hearing Hank's final performance on the show. I distinctly recall him making a very low-key farewell speech...in fact, I wasn't really sure of what I was hearing. He simply casually mentioned that he had enjoyed his time at the Opry but he was going to take some time to relax...and that was it. He did his final song and he was gone. No fanfare, no big to-do...but very much in keeping with his somewhat reticent style. When you think about it, it's kind of sad that little was said about a forty-six-year run.

Jimmie recalls that while the family knew it was difficult for him to retire from the Opry, they also recognized that the time had come—and he's sure that Hank knew it as well.

> Performing on the Opry was important to him, so much so that he practised every night right up until he left in 1996. By then, he was starting to get frail and he knew it was time to step back...we knew it too. He always said

Hank retired from touring in 1985 to spend time with his wife, Minnie.

if he ever got to the place where performing became difficult for him then he would call it quits so that's what he did. He had enough sense about him to realize something was wrong with him, but giving up the Opry was hard for him. It was a big part of his life.

Sheri Blackwood, remembers that time leading up to Hank's retirement and notes that as Hank was getting older, his glaucoma was getting worse and he was constantly putting drops in his eyes. "This was around 1992 or 1993, and he had begun working on his book. He had two writers to do the work but he wanted to put it in his own words. He sat at the typewriter day after day getting down everything he could remember…page after page and sending it to them. He was always sharing stories with me. It was like he was frantic to get it all down. It needed to be documented."

When the manuscript was sent to Hank, Sheri read it to him. "We would read a few pages and it would remind Hank of other stories. And when the book was published in 1994, I sat in the office and read the complete book again to him. We both enjoyed that. I was fortunate to have that experience. I was re-living Hank's entire life and career right there with him."

Hank's book was published in 1994 and Sheri believes it was later that year that they started seeing the first signs of dementia.

> We didn't recognize it as such but as time went on it was obvious something very serious was happening. He began cancelling his Opry appearances…. It was getting more and more frequent…. It was a real problem for the people at the Opry because Hank was a regular host on the 9:30 P.M. and 11 P.M. Saturday night Grand Ole Opry, along with hosting shows on the Friday night Opry. He would never tell anyone (not even me) until two or three hours before the show that he was not going to be there. He never gave a reason and would never say he didn't feel well…just that he had decided not to do the show. It was a real problem for everyone—the Opry staff would already have the programs printed—the band members were just on standby until they received a call from me. It wasn't easy for anyone, but Hank called the shots. It wasn't long before the rumours started circulating that Hank was drinking again. Of course this was absolutely false. Hank had not had a drink since he quit in the early '70s.

Sheri recalls it was a tough time.

> I could see Hank was sick. As time went on, it wasn't getting any better and from all indications it was not

going to get better. There were days he would not come into the office. He would stay in bed all day and talk to me on the intercom. The office phone rang in his bedroom and when I was not there, Hank would sometimes answer. He would make appointments without telling me and when people would show up at the gate, Hank would have me tell them that he wasn't available. People just didn't understand that rejection after they had driven all the way out to the office expecting to see Hank.

After missing many of his Opry shows between 1995 and 1996, Hank made one last appearance in 1996. "He always said he would know when it was time to leave, not just the Opry but the music business in general. And he did. He stopped touring a few years before this and he knew it was time for him to leave the Opry. September 6, 1996, would be the last appearance on the Opry that Hank would make."

A Life in Show Business

Despite all of Hank's success, all his accolades and awards, and all his fame, the emotional scars from the abuse he endured as a child stayed with him his entire life. The physical marks may have healed, but he could never forget the pain he suffered at the hands of people he'd trusted, people who should have loved him and cared for him. When he finally had the means, he decided to do something to help other abused and neglected children.

In 1976, spurred on by the horrific story of a five-year-old girl from Cleveland, Tennessee, who was abused and killed by her stepfather, Hank organized a benefit concert with the aid of other Grand Ole Opry talent. He would raise money to establish a shelter for abused children. That effort raised seventeen thousand dollars and Hank was so inspired by the response that he wanted to do more. A year later, he founded the Hank Snow Foundation for the Prevention of Child Abuse and Neglect, International. Its goal was to build a centre to help children in distress by giving them safe shelter while also providing training programs for counsellors to work with parents.

While the early years of the foundation were successful ones, Hank struggled to keep it going for seven years through benefit concerts and donations. When it became too much for Hank to handle, largely because of his busy schedule, he turned the operation over to the Exchange Clubs of America. Hank remained on the board for several more years in an advisory capacity while using his celebrity status and impressive network of contacts to help raise funds aimed at keeping the programs going, but seven years later he had to step away as demands for his time became too difficult to juggle.

Throughout the remainder of his life, Hank was devoted to eradicating childhood abuse and neglect, lending his voice and celebrity status to fighting these crimes whenever he could. In time, he and Minnie also became involved with the Christian Children's Fund, through which they sponsored many overseas children and promoted the cause of the organization.

Being able to help people in need was one of the perks of fame that Hank most appreciated. And there certainly were others, but as Hank was quick to point out, a life in show business is not all fun and glamour. In truth, it's a lot of hard work that requires sacrifice, and contrary to what people may think, life for an entertainer, especially a singer who has to spend time on the road touring to support his music, is not easy. But despite some difficult times, Hank never complained about it, nor would he ever have traded it for another profession. After all, he had worked extremely hard to reach the level of success he had achieved, and while there were times when circumstances knocked him down, or when he was tired and felt like quitting, Hank Snow persevered.

Hank always felt that entertaining people was what he was meant to do and he could not even imagine what his life would have been like without music in it, or the chance to perform in front of an audience. It was an amazing adventure, he said, adding that he felt he had been truly blessed. Hank believed that his talent was a God-given gift, but his drive and determination to achieve success were all his. He admitted that he may have occasionally veered from that path over the years, but somehow, with the support of people he

Hank Snow during a performance at Toronto's
Roy Thomson Hall in the 1970s.

loved, he always found his way back to that road and pushed forward with a new-found determination. Somehow, no matter the size of the challenge or the breadth of the sacrifice, Hank Snow kept his faith and stayed focused on his goal of someday becoming an international recording star.

When asked what he thought was the greatest challenge he faced on his rise to stardom, Hank would say there were too many to simply pick one, but he pointed out that when times got difficult, his answer was to keep his faith, draw inspiration from the love and support of his family and friends who believed in him, and remain focused on his ultimate goal, which was to make music that people would like. He achieved that and more.

Hank realized his dream, sometimes through nothing more than sheer determination and true grit, possibly achieving success even greater than he could have ever imagined. Ultimately, he became a legend in country music, reaching heights that only a select few could match. With a string of hits, records selling into the millions, worldwide tours, critical acclaim, and a long list of awards, at the height of his success Hank Snow was literally a household name throughout North America and beyond.

Did he ever have doubts or second thoughts about what he was doing? Of course he did. The life of a travelling entertainer is not an easy one. Hank admitted that the smiling, energetic singer and guitar player that audiences saw on the stage wasn't always the real Hank Snow, but people had paid to see him perform and he was committed to giving it his best shot no matter what. That meant sometimes even going on stage when he was tired and sick and could hardly stand straight, but he still managed to perform. To him, a concert was like a contract between the audience and the entertainer and he felt obligated to give them the show they expected. For Hank, giving his fans what they wanted was the ultimate payoff.

Hank was constantly asked throughout his career how many songs he had recorded and how many albums he had released over the years. While he admitted he had never really kept track of those numbers, he estimated he had recorded over one thousand songs throughout his career, and between his RCA records in the U.S. and the seventy-five he recorded in Canada on the Bluebird label, he believed he had released over seven hundred songs. It was estimated that from 1936 to 1974, when he signed a new contract with RCA, Hank Snow had sold more than 86 million records. His hit "I'm Movin' On" is considered by many industry insiders to be one of the most influential and successful country music songs of all time, and still holds many international records for its longevity on the charts. Not bad for a skinny and sickly poor boy from rural Nova Scotia.

Hank's influence on other artists is well documented, but some stories, such as his involvement with Baltimore-based singer-songwriter Mark Brine, are not. Successful artists are often asked by aspiring singers to help in their efforts or to do them some favours, and Hank received many requests from up-and-comers to help them get on the Opry. And it's not that successful artists don't want to help these individuals—because Hank admitted he owed his place at the Opry to the efforts of his friend Ernest Tubb—it's just that they often don't have the time to do it or that the demands are just too much to accommo-date. Hank was no different from any of the other country superstars, but occasionally, when he recognized talent or a certain "spark," he would sometimes lend a helping hand. Such was Mark's case.

Sometime early in 1992, Mark, an aspiring singer-songwriter, sent Hank a 45 rpm version of a song he had written and recorded, called "New Blue Yodel." The flip side was a song called "Blues In My Mind," and honestly, Mark says, he believed it was a long shot that Hank Snow would even listen to the record, which was written in honour of the late Jimmie Rodgers, and he certainly never expected that he would ever hear from the legendary singer. But in March or April 1992, with no warning, Hank phoned Mark at his home, catch-ing him totally by surprise.

"He called to say he loved the record, being a huge Jimmie Rodgers fan, and commended me on it," Mark recalls. "We talked a good while. He asked about my Nashville Days [1974 to 1985] and I told him that I ultimately left to record in New York where I could be myself. But I told him my only regret was that I'd never gotten to play the Opry, as I went there to be like him and Hank Williams. I told him I was traditional country and he said, 'Let me see what I can do.'"

Mark admits that when Hank hung up the phone following their conversation, he didn't think he'd ever hear from him again. However, he adds, "When I was touring in Switzerland—it was May or June— [Hank] called my wife, Karen, in Baltimore and gave her the date for my 'debut' on the Grand Ole Opry. I couldn't believe that he had actually arranged for me to appear on the Opry."

But both Jimmie and Sheri agree that Hank did more to help other people than anyone really knew, because he didn't go around promoting his good deeds.

"That's not why he did it," Jimmie points out.

"There was so much more to Hank than people knew," Sheri says. "He did so much that he didn't want people to know about be-cause that's what Hank was like. I saw him do many wonderful things that made me proud to call him my friend."

THE END OF THE ROAD

The Twilight Years

In his book, *The Hank Snow Story*, Snow writes:

> Overall, friends, I must say that my whole career has
> been highly rewarding. I've played in many parts of the
> world to all kinds of audiences...I've sung songs to the
> working people and to presidents, to poor people and to
> royalty. Even with the hard travelling, I wouldn't have
> missed it for the world....Who would have thought that
> an abused little boy, with less than a fifth grade educa-
> tion, and living at times in the depths of poverty, would
> achieve every goal that he ever dreamed of? The Good
> Lord has sure been good to me.

From his first recording session with RCA Victor in Montreal
in 1936 to his last Nashville recording session at RCA in November
1980, Hank Snow recorded a total of 833 songs and 104 albums. Up
until his last Saturday night performance at the Grand Ole Opry
House on August 31, 1996, and his final Friday night show a week
later on September 6, Hank continued to do his half-hour show every
week. He was ready to retire.

By 1999 Hank's health was deteriorating very rapidly. Sheri
Blackwood remembers:

Hank Snow on stage at the Grand Ole Opry, 1993.

Things were getting really bad.... Not too many good
days. Although there was one day in July that year that
I will never forget. Hank called me and asked what I was
doing. I told him that I was leaving to run out to West
Nashville and pick up a prescription for my dad. He asked
me to stop by and get him. He wanted to go out to Clyde's
[his barber] for a haircut. When I arrived at his house he
was dressed and ready to go. It was the greatest conversation all the way. He enjoyed his visit with Clyde...he

hadn't seen him in a while. On the way back, he wanted
to make a few stops to handle some personal business.
It was the best day I could remember in a long time.... It
was like he had made this miraculous recovery. He was
joking around, just like the old Hank. I couldn't believe
it. I was thrilled.... But that was short lived.

About three months before Hank's death, Sheri recalls that she
received an urgent request from a caller in Liverpool.

He needed to talk to Hank but was unable to reach him
on the phone. By that time, Hank had secluded himself inside his home. The request was from the family
of a lady—a close friend from Hank's past—who had
a terminal illness and was given only a short time to
live. Her dying wish was to receive a note from Hank.
Since I was just about the only one allowed to pass the
barrier of his gates and get inside the residence, I told
him I would deliver the message.

And she did.

We sat in his living room. Hank was in his favourite
recliner and I was sitting on the couch across from him,
notebook in hand. The words came easily for him. He
couldn't have been more comforting if he had been
standing by [the woman's] bedside. I asked how he
wanted to close it out. True to form, Hank lightheart-
edly waved his hand in the air and said, "Au revoir!
Leave the light on for me." We didn't put that in the
note, but thinking back perhaps we should have. She
obviously knew Hank well. And that's a comment that
would have been expected of him.

Sheri remembers that her last "real" conversation with Hank
was Thanksgiving Day 1999.

My husband and I were preparing to go to my parents' for the holiday and Hank's caregiver, Michelle, placed the call for him. He was in a good mood...happy...and wanted to wish us a happy Thanksgiving. He sent messages to my parents and my brothers; he remembered everyone by name. Min was home and they had a Thanksgiving dinner planned. It was wonderful to hear him so happy. But after that, throughout the next month, things changed.

After that, Sheri's only visits with Hank would be at the hospital.

Following his retirement from the Grand Ole Opry, Hank devoted a great deal of time to promoting his book, *The Hank Snow Story*, an effort that brought him much personal satisfaction. Jimmie recalls, "Since he had given up touring and he was no longer performing, the book became his whole life—and what a life it was." The effort became an appropriate closing chapter to the life of a man who overcame so many seemingly insurmountable odds to see his dreams become reality; a man who rose from meagre and humble roots to become one of the true legends of country and western music.

The last few years of Hank's life, much of which he spent secluded at Rainbow Ranch, were dominated by his failing health. "People may not realize that Dad was 145 pounds his entire adult life, so he was always a slight man as far as build goes," Jimmie says. "He

Hank at work behind his desk in his home office.

was only five feet, six inches tall, and that's why he wore cowboy boots all the time because they made him taller. It was no wonder then when he started to get sick, that he quickly became frail."

Jimmie had always remembered his father as a healthy person most of his life. "When he got sick it was really hard to see him that way, and with him, because of his build, you could really notice the change. In the end, he suffered from dementia and that made him really paranoid, which really wasn't typical of him as he was always pretty sharp. But, for instance, he had three locks installed on all the doors and he'd roam around the house in his housecoat carrying a gun in his pocket, that's how paranoid he became."

Hank worried a great deal, Jimmie explains.

> That caused him to develop bleeding ulcers. To deal with that he went into the hospital and had them cauterized, but he was getting really sick by that time. The situation got worse when he was eating a meal at home after that procedure and he aspirated some food into his lungs. That, in turn, led to pneumonia, and although his death certificate lists the cause of death as a heart attack, it was actually the pneumonia that killed him. An autopsy confirmed all of this.

Once Hank developed pneumonia he was hospitalized for a while, where doctors and nurses watched over him until eventually, Jimmie says, it became obvious that the end was near.

> After they told us his chances for recovery were not good and they outlined all the options for us, like putting him on a feeding tube, Mother and I felt Dad wouldn't want to be kept alive like that. They told us at the hospital that a feeding tube would be painful for him and considering his age it might be too much for him. I just didn't think that was the right thing to do, so we said no to the tube and brought him home. We felt he would want to spend whatever time he had left back at Rainbow Ranch. We put him in a separate room next

to the living room and with the help of hospice work-
ers from the hospital, who stayed with him around the
clock, we kept him at home and cared for him there.

Jimmie admits this was a difficult time for the family.

"Mother could not go into the room to see him like that, but I
spent a lot of time with him. You have to understand that Dad and I never talked much, not even when I was a child. He just wasn't that kind
of parent and he never hugged anyone. He just didn't do it but I knew
he loved me." By the time the family brought him home, Hank was no
longer able to communicate, but one day, maybe ten days before he
died, he asked Jimmie if he could fix his pillow. "And as I reached down
to do that, he gave me a hug.... It was the last time we communicated."

Somehow, defying medical opinion, Hank managed to stay
alive for several weeks, but—and Jimmie says, "I remember this very
clearly"—on Hank's last day, Jimmie just happened to walk into his
father's room when all of a sudden the elder Snow sat up straight in
his bed and stared off into the heavens. "He didn't say anything, but
then he just laid his head back down on his pillow and slipped away.
He went very peacefully. It was very quiet but I am glad I was there
with him at the end."

Hank Snow died at 12:18 A.M., December 20, 1999, at his home
in Madison, Tennessee. He was eighty-five.

On December 21, 1999, newspaper headlines around the world
declared the news of Hank Snow's death. The Halifax *Chronicle
Herald* ran a front-page story with the headline "Snow dead at 85."
The *Toronto Star* proclaimed "Hank Snow moves on," while the
Toronto Sun went with a similar headline, reading "Snow movin'
on: Country legend Hank dies at 85." The front-page lead story in
Nashville's newspaper, *The Tennessean*, announced, "Country music
legend Hank Snow moves on: Opry pillar is dead at 85."

In *The Tennessean* article by Jay Orr and Robert K. Oermann,
Opry House manager Jerry Strobel is quoted as saying: "In the his-
tory of country music, Hank would be considered one of those pillars
of the Grand Ole Opry along with legends Roy Acuff, Bill Monroe,
Minnie Pearl, Grandpa Jones, and Ernest Tubb." Strobel continued:
"Hank was one of the most professional entertainers I've ever met. He

would rehearse with his group before each Opry performance even though he might have sang the song 1,000 times before. He would also want to make sure that his introduction of an artist, whether it was a regular cast member or a guest, was precise and laudatory."

Kyle Young, a director of the Country Music Hall of Fame in Nashville, was quoted in the same article. "He was one of the earliest inductees," Young said of Hank, who was enshrined in the Hall of Fame in 1979. "When I think about him, I think about his versatility. He was a distinctive stylist and one of the best songwriters in the history of country music."

Also quoted was fellow Opry cast member Jean Shepard, who shared a dressing room with Hank for many years. "He was a master in the business," she said. "He was a great stylist. The minute you heard something by Hank Snow, you knew exactly who it was. Those people are few and far between. He sold more records than most that are on record today and this was fifty years ago."

In the *Toronto Star* article, writer Greg Quill quoted Nashville musicologist Chas Wolfe: "He was the first truly international country music star. Americans still don't know how enormously popular Hank Snow was in Canada in the 1930s and '40s and as far away as Australia in the 1950s, where he was huge."

As is the custom with every member of the Grand Ole Opry, funeral services for Hank Snow were held at the legendary venue on Thursday, December 23, 1999. A report in *The Tennessean* about the three-hour service, by writer Jay Orr, noted that Jimmie Rodgers's old railroad lantern was lit in honour of Hank Snow. For an hour before the service, attendees filed by the open casket to pay their respects to the country music legend who had been just a month short of celebrating his fiftieth anniversary at the Opry when he died. "Marty Stuart brought the lantern to the Opry House where several hundred mourners, including family, friends, fans and musical colleagues paid tribute to Mr. Snow," the article read. "Stuart placed the lantern given to him by Mr. Snow, near the casket before performing several songs from Mr. Snow's repertoire."

Rev. Jimmie Rodgers Snow, Hank's son, presided over the service, while Stuart played Hank's guitar and performed two of Hank's biggest hits, "(Now and Then There's) A Fool Such As I" and "I Don't

Hank's memorial service at the Grand Ole Opry on December 23, 1999.

Hurt Anymore." When Stuart finished performing, he placed the guitar on a stand next to a sparkling stage costume, white with blue trim.

Speaking at the ceremony and sharing their memories of their friend were many other country music legends, including long-time Canadian Tommy Hunter, who had befriended Hank years earlier, and other Opry stars such as Johnny Russell and Porter Wagoner. Connie Smith performed "Peace in the Valley" and led the attendees in "Amazing Grace." Billy Walker performed "Fallen Leaves," a song closely connected to Hank's friend Grandpa Jones, and "I Will See You in the Rapture." Contemporary artist Steve Wariner performed his hit, "Holes in the Floor of Heaven," John Berry sang "Blessed Assurance," and The Hemphills gospel group closed the service with "The Only Real Peace." Members of The Rainbow Ranch Boys, including Kayton Roberts, Hank's long-time steel guitar player, also performed.

The list of attendees at the service included a mixture of legendary country artists, such as Little Jimmy Dickens, Jeanne Pruett, Johnnie Wright, Jeannie Seely, Jan Howard and Kitty Wells, and more contemporary stars such as Garth Brooks and The Whites.

Speaking at the service, Stuart said, "Hank Snow was a great folk hero and one of the first international stars. The dignity of country music—a huge part of it—lies in front of us today." Following the ceremony, Hank Snow was interred in the Spring Hill Cemetery in Nashville, Tennessee.

Minnie Blanche (Aalders) Snow, wife of Hank Snow, died Monday, May 12, 2003, of complications from pneumonia at Vanderbilt University Medical Center in Nashville. She was eighty-nine. News reports at the time confirmed she had been sick for several years and had recently been battling cancer. Following a respectful service attended by family and close friends, she was laid to rest next to her husband at the Spring Hill Cemetery.

Remembering Hank Snow

Canadian country music legend Tommy Hunter said of Hank Snow following Hank's death, "He had a very distinctive voice, a deep, beautiful voice. Hank was a great guy and certainly a character. There was a sense of humour that very few people ever saw in Hank, but he could be very, very funny." He also referred to the renowned singer as an accomplished narrator and instrumentalist. "I know no other artist in this business who has bridged all three of those." Speaking at Snow's funeral service, he added, "Canadians love Hank Snow like no other native son, that I can tell you. He's a legend from one end of the country to the other."

Looking back over his father's life, Jimmie Rodgers Snow had this to say:

> I would like for Dad to be remembered as one of the true pioneers of country music, who not only paved the way for other Canadian performers who came along after him, but also for country music artists in general. Today, you wouldn't have the Keith Urbans, Tim McGraws, and Kenny Chesneys if it wasn't for pioneers like Dad, people who knocked down barriers and took

country music to new audiences at a time when country music wasn't popular. He came to a place in the world that didn't know anything about Nova Scotia but he worked hard and gave up a lot. He was so driven that when he set his mind to something there was no stopping him, and that's how he achieved his dreams of becoming a country music singer.

Even though Hank eventually became an American citizen and lived in Nashville for the better part of his life, Jimmie says his father never forgot his Canadian roots, especially his Nova Scotian home. Hank credited many of the life lessons he learned while he was growing up in Brooklyn and Liverpool—as well as Lunenburg and Halifax—during the Depression for giving him the strength, fortitude, and courage to go after what he wanted.

The one thing Jimmie remembered most about his father was that he was a driven man: he had to be to make it in the entertainment business. "After all, here was a man who only had a grade five education, which meant he was basically self-taught. Pretty much everything he knew he figured out on his own. That's just how it was back then. It was a different way of life from what we expect today and Dad was trying to make it in a business that wasn't an easy road to travel."

While conceding that, at times, his father may have seemed more focused on his career than on his family, Jimmie says he and his mother were never neglected. But they did have many struggles.

Hank Snow in his later years.

People might think that after we moved to Nashville and Dad started appearing on the Opry, things got easier for us, but they really didn't. It was still a struggle for us and times were still tough. He was playing the Opry but he wasn't exactly setting the world on fire. Even though he was pretty well known in Canada, it was a different story in the U.S., where not many people knew the name Hank Snow. After "I'm Movin' On" came out in 1950, the world became a different place for us. That song changed everything for Dad, for us and for country music. At twenty-one, the song still holds the record for spending the most consecutive weeks at number one on the charts. Once that song became such a big hit, we were able to move out of the tiny rental house in 1951. We moved into the larger house that Dad called Rainbow Ranch. We went from one thousand square feet to 3,600 square feet on three acres of land and we started buying nice things and fancy cars. It was a whole new world for us.

Despite the early struggles, though, Jimmie says he wouldn't have changed anything. He travelled, which meant he got to see a lot of the world and had lots of unique experiences. His lifestyle and that of his father's also meant he got to meet many famous and interesting people.

My childhood was basically an education. Looking back at my life now as an adult, I don't begrudge any of it. It was tough and we struggled, but when you look back over your own life, you have to ask yourself if it was worth it. I think, for Dad, it was worth it. He worked hard all his life and came from a place that no one had ever heard of to become a worldwide celebrity. That's a major accomplishment. I can't hold that against him, but I do have two regrets—that I was an only child and that we didn't have a normal father-son relationship. I can't help but think I missed out on a lot as a child, but he made up for it in many other ways.

Throughout his career, Hank had many talented musicians join him on stage and on record and a select group of those became members of his band, which he called The Rainbow Ranch Boys. As of 2014, only two of those band members remained alive—his long-time steel guitar player, Kayton Roberts, and his bass player, Roger Carol. Each summer, both men travel to Nova Scotia to participate in the annual Hank Snow Tribute, an annual music festival, which has been held in various South Shore locations starting at Summerville Beach in 1991 and moving to Caledonia the next year and then to Bridgewater as attendance grew. In 2013 the Tribute moved to Liverpool.

When Kayton Roberts arrived in Nashville in 1967, good fortune smiled on him and he landed a job with Hank Snow. It was the best gig he ever could have hoped for. He has many fond memories of his travels with Hank and of making music with the legendary entertainer. "We had some great musicians in the band and they were fun to play with, but Hank was great to perform with. He was a consummate professional who expected the best from the guys and he'd let you know if you let him down in any way."

Although Kayton is known as Hank's steel guitar player, most people are surprised to learn that he actually started in the band playing rhythm guitar for about a year until Hank's regular steel guitar player left for another job. "After that, Hank put me on steel guitar and I played with him for the rest of his life."

On the career of Hank Snow, Kayton says there is no other way to describe the man except as a legend.

> Hank Snow is a legend and may have been one of the greatest songwriters of all time. Just look at the songs he wrote, even those he wrote in Canada before he came to the States were great. The fact that Hank was Canadian never got in the way of anything for him. The truth was, Hank's success was all about talent and he had an ample supply of that. Hank was also a great guitar player and I think he was one of the greatest—if not the greatest—guitar players of all time.

People will always remember Hank Snow. They loved him and he left a mark that changed country music forever. Hank never forgot where he came from and he talked a lot about his earlier days growing up in Nova Scotia and the struggles he had. He didn't mind talking about the bad times because he said they made him the person that he was. He said times were tough and sometimes that's good because it makes you appreciate what you get when you do finally get it.

Despite some of the rough edges that those tough times may have given Hank, Kayton says, "Hank had many good qualities as well," and Kayton has nothing but fond memories of his time with the legendary entertainer. While some people found Hank to be set in his ways and sometimes difficult to deal with because he seemed to be so focused on what he wanted, Kayton attributes that personality trait to the man's drive and determination to succeed.

In this business you could end up working for anyone, but when you end up working for a man of the stature of Hank Snow, that is special right there. As his band, we were in the limelight. You knew that and if you play an instrument in Nashville, that's exactly where you want to be. As far as I was concerned, it was like a baseball player going to the major leagues. I can stand up and say I played with Hank Snow and I was proud of it and most people would know who he was...even younger people today would know who he was.

Roger Carol also has many fond memories of working with Hank. From Springfield, Tennessee, just north of Nashville, Roger had been listening to Hank Snow records for many years before pursuing a career in country music, and in fact it was people like Hank Snow who inspired the young musician to pursue a career in the business in the first place. A talented guitar player, Roger got the job with Hank in the spring of 1979 at age twenty-six on a recommendation from Kayton, who had previously heard Roger play and suggested him to Hank when an opening came up in the band. Roger remembers the circumstances very well.

"Just like yesterday," Roger smiles.

> I talked to Hank and he had me come over to the Opry where he was playing on the weekend. After he had me try out, he told me to come back the next week and he had someone send me the uniform that the Rainbow Ranch Boys had to wear. Hank Snow was known for his flashy stage outfits and his band was expected to wear the uniform Hank provided...if you didn't, you didn't play. It was as simple as that. I had my uniform adjusted to fit me and I just kept going back week after week, but, actually, Hank never told me I had the job. After three years of playing with him, I finally asked one day if I got the job. He looked at me and said, "I'm still thinking about it but you're kind of on thin ice." He made a joke of it, but that's how I started playing with Hank and that lasted twenty years. He never would tell me officially, though, that I had the job, but the cheques kept coming.

Playing in Hank Snow's band was a great opportunity, Roger says. "I was really honoured to get to join the band because by that time Hank Snow was already a legend in country music. Think about the timing—I started playing with Hank in the spring of 1979 and that fall he went into the Hall of Fame. That's impressive, and it was a thrill to work for a man like that."

Playing with Hank Snow at the Grand Ole Opry would thrill any musician, Roger adds. "I remember the first time taking the stage of the Opry with Hank. Our first song was 'Ramblin' Rose.' I can't tell you what that was like. It was a very humbling experience...just standing there on that stage watching these guys [the band] play. They're all legends in their own right and as the newcomer, you feel pretty small."

There is no question in Roger's mind that today's artists owe a great debt to people like Hank Snow. "Listen to today's music. You can hear Hank's influence on many of today's artists. He broke down many doors and country music wouldn't be where it is today without people like Hank Snow who did so much for the music in the earlier years."

Sometimes, Roger says, he felt Hank didn't get the recognition he deserved, especially as a guitar player.

> Hank had some great skills as a guitar player. I think people just took him for granted, but people were more influenced by Hank Snow then they realized. In a town where there's Chet Atkins and people like that, it's easy to get overshadowed. Although Hank and Chet did some really great music together and recorded a couple of great albums, I'm not sure people gave Hank the credit for the fine instrumentalist that he was. Usually, when people mention great guitar players in Nashville, they mentioned the greats like Chet Atkins and that's very well deserved because he was great, but Hank was right up there with him in every way. Maybe he wasn't so well known as a guitar player because he was better known as a singer, songwriter and entertainer.... And as a person, he was professional and private and really great to work for. It truly was an honour to be a part of Hank Snow's legacy.

Another person with memories of Hank Snow is Canada's Queen of Country Music, Carroll Baker, who coincidentally also hails from Nova Scotia's South Shore. Although born in Bridgewater, she is proud to say she is from Port Medway. Herself an award-winning singer with a legion of fans, she remembered when Hank was a guest on her CBC TV special, "Carroll Baker In Nashville," in 1979, and she said she found him to be very warm, accommodating, and fun to work with.

"When I was doing my special in Nashville, [Hank] asked if he could go and see the portion of the show that was being taped from the Grand Ole Opry House," she recalls. "We were very excited about the chance to have him there and on the day of the taping, he showed up backstage and asked someone to take him to his seat in the audience as he didn't know how to get out to the audience. He told us he had never sat in the theatre part of the Opry, only backstage. It was his birthday and he changed his plans to go see me at the Opry."

Hank Snow and Carroll Baker at Rainbow Ranch in 1979,
during the taping of her CBC television special.

Carroll was honoured that Hank would do that and she also recalls that some time later, she met him again at the Opry during a
Saturday night show. "I had been invited back to perform on the Opry
as a special guest and it worked out that I appeared on the part of the
show that Hank was hosting. I did my song and got an encore, and he
went on at great length telling the audience about the TV special that
he did with me and that he was very impressed by it. That meant a lot."

One other person with a close insight into Hank Snow is his
good friend Marge Hemsworth, who lives in Halifax but maintained a
close bond with Hank and Minnie for many years. She says her association with the legendary singer goes way back. "Some people would

even say our connection is somewhat convoluted," she laughs, "but they were both very good friends and I miss them dearly."

Marge's association with Hank began when she was eleven years old. "I heard on CHNS that Hank was down at Phinney's Record shop. So off we went on our lunch hour from school and there he was. He was very gracious. He took my arm and stood me by him for the photographer.... I was star-struck."

This was the winter of 1948 and the beginning of a close friendship. Marge admitted that she may have been enamoured with Hank's rising star status, but she thought he was a wonderful singer and a friendly man who always took the time to talk with his fans. "In 1956 when I was 18 and was working, I was walking home on my lunch hour when I saw the three Snows outside of CHNS. I stopped and talked to Min. She was very nice. That was July and shortly after that, a friend and I went to Nashville for the first time."

It was the first of many trips she would take to Nashville.

"We were having breakfast in this small diner when Marty Robbins came over and joined us. He just sat down and started talking to us. He was very nice and when we told him we were from Nova Scotia, he told us Hank, who was the star of *Noontime Neighbors*, was taping right next door at WSM Studio C and he was there right now if we wanted to come over and say hi....so we did."

Marge said it was an amazing experience and Hank was very gracious.

> When we got there, he came right over and said, "Hi, ladies. How are things in Halifax?" It was amazing because he really didn't know us at that time. We said, "How did you know we were from Halifax?" and he said, "You were outside CHNS talking to my wife." He remembered us and that says a lot about the kind of person that Hank was. To think that he could remember us among all the people that he would meet really left a lasting impression on me.

That night, Marge recalled, she and her friend went back to see Hank Snow perform on the *Friday Night Frolics* in Studio C. The next day they went to Rainbow Ranch for a visit and then Hank took them

Hank with Marge Hemsworth in the 1950s.

to the Grand Ole Opry that night so they could watch his show. "It was a great experience and Hank and Minnie were gracious hosts," she says, noting that over the years, she went to Nashville many times to visit the Snows. "You could not ask for any nicer people."

Over the years, Marge had the opportunity to meet many country music legends through her friendship with Hank, but she quickly added that none of them could hold a candle to Hank.

"Maybe it was because we were both from Nova Scotia, but we seemed to connect and he and his family were very special people in my life," she says, adding that at times Hank would often confide in her when things weren't always going the way he thought they should. In particular, she smiles, he would sometimes ask her why some people said he was difficult to get along with.

I'd laugh and say, "Because you are." He'd just look at me and smirk, but he knew what I meant. But I understood what it was like for him. He was under a great deal of pressure all the time and it can't be easy to be in the public limelight like that. I basically told him that no matter how difficult things became, he had to remember that whenever he was in public, people would be scrutinizing him so he always had to be on his best behaviour. He just took it in stride and did his own thing, but that's what Hank was really like. I don't think he worried too much about the approval of other people. He was a hard worker, a devoted family man, a talented performer, a dear friend, and a trailblazer.

When Hank Snow died in 1999, Marge says the world not only lost a legendary singer-songwriter, but she lost a very close friend. "There are many other entertainers out there, but there will only ever be one Hank Snow, and the fact that he was from Nova Scotia makes him all the more special."

Behind the Scenes

Hank Snow's accomplishments are, indeed, legendary. His signature song, "I'm Movin' On," is now considered a country music standard that, at last count, has been recorded in thirty-six languages. Impressive indeed, but for people who were close to him, none of that success changed the man. Most agree that Hank Snow remained humble throughout his career, despite a reputation as a perfectionist and being difficult to work with. Although such labels may have sometimes described Hank when he was at his worst, for the most part they weren't accurate descriptions of the entertainer or the man. In fact, those who knew him insist that Hank's drive and determination to succeed in the very demanding entertainment business gave him a hard edge that may have sometimes been misinterpreted or misunderstood, and his tough past also likely influenced his disposition.

Sheri Blackwood, Hank's personal assistant for over twenty-seven years, knew him on a professional level; but more than that, she was his friend. Working in her office located in Hank's home, she got to see him as a boss, a businessman, an entertainer, a family man, a friend, and as a singer-songwriter who was deeply devoted to his fans. "I was nineteen when I started working for Hank and I worked for him until around 1995. My dad was in bad health and this was about the time when things were starting to get a little more complicated in Hank's life, but I stayed close and was in and out frequently up until his death in 1999."

Sheri speaks as someone who knew Hank very well.

> I literally shared an office with him. We were in the same room. I was there for all his telephone conversations, his interviews, and even went with him to many

of his meetings outside the office. Just through the glass doors from our office and studio was his main residence. Hank was friends with some of the richest and most famous people in the world. He could pick up the phone and get through to anybody he wanted to talk to. They would always take a call from Hank Snow.

At home, Sheri recalls, Hank was relaxed, but he always stayed busy because he enjoyed his work.

He had routines that he would follow like clockwork. He worked late into the night in his studio and slept late in the morning. He'd come into the office usually around 11 A.M. He ate one meal a day...every day promptly at 5 P.M. When the intercom sounded and he was asked what he wanted for supper it was something like one strip of bacon or one small piece of ham, one egg and one slice of toast. Or he would order six ears of boiled corn.... That one I couldn't believe. He often ate fish. He had his seafood flown in from Boston. He knew what he wanted and was very specific about it. Hank's weakness was sweets...all the way up until bedtime he was munching, and sometimes even after he went to bed. I think he forced regular food down just because he felt he needed it to stay healthy...and to take his vitamins with. He took about thirty vitamins daily. But he never exercised.

Hank always made lists, she remembers.

He always had a list in progress in his shirt pocket. He put everything on there. When he was at his desk he was making notes all the time. He'd tear the list off and put it in his pocket. If he was in his chair in the living room, he would be staring out the window and then he would take the list and write something. Usually first thing when he came in to the office in the morning he would transfer everything that had not been marked off

Sheri Blackwood and Hank Snow at work in his home office.

to the new list. Everything went on the list—wash the car, clean jewelry, fuel the bus, tell a joke—whatever, it all went on the list.

Sheri also recalls that Hank was superstitious when it came to travelling. "He would never leave to go on the road on a Friday. It was bad luck! If he had to leave on Friday, it would be a few minutes after midnight or, if necessary, he would leave on Thursday night." He also liked reading, and according to Sheri, the book that meant the most to Hank during his life was *Think and Grow Rich*. He'd read it at least a dozen times.

Hank enjoyed success stories. His favourite, or at least the one he talked about most often, was the life of Henry Ford. He enjoyed the part where they had him in court trying to have him declared incompetent and when asked how he would handle certain issues, he said "I don't clutter my brain with things like that. I have people who handle that for me. If I want to know something I just press a button!" Hank loved that.

In addition to reading, Sheri says, later on, when he had more time, Hank watched a lot of TV; in particular he watched *The World at War* several times. "He enjoyed movies, but he absolutely couldn't get enough of *Three's Company*. He knew John Ritter personally and wouldn't miss a single episode. He taped every single one of them over the years. If I missed it, he had it on tape for me to watch the next day. If there was one show that was his favourite, that was it."

The quirky things stand out for Sheri.

> He was always doing something to entertain himself. Once he was target shooting at a can set up on the bus ramp from the office step. He missed and shot a hole in his truck.... He would get bored very easily. He would shoot paper wads during a telephone interview because he said he had answered the same questions for so many years. One question he especially didn't like to answer was when he was asked why he wrote certain songs. He said the main reason was, "Because I was hungry."

She recalls one day when Hank was doing a live "on-the-air" telephone interview.

> Hank was a professional and nothing was ever rehearsed with him. He was so relaxed, whether it was live or taped. He didn't even think about what he was going to say. But on this day, for some reason he decided to throw in a little Bible quote and without realizing he had gotten his quotes mixed up, he said, "Like it says in the Bible—what goes around comes around." After that, we always gave Hank credit for that quote when we used it. It would be, "Like Hank says, like it says in the Bible...."

After that, Sheri always left reminders on Hank's desk before interviews. "And he would say, 'I know, I know. Don't quote the Bible.'"

Hank was known to have a colourful vocabulary, Sheri says. "That was just Hank. But he always looked up and asked forgiveness on the spot if he actually took the Lord's name in vain."

By this time, Hank's son, Jimmie, had a large church in Madison, which was attended by many country music celebrities. Hank truly admired Jimmie's knowledge of the Bible," Sheri says.

> He would say, "Jimmie knows the Bible better than anyone and he's a great teacher...his delivery is the best I've heard." Hank didn't go to church, but he was to some extent a very spiritual person. I know things would get on his mind and he would often call Jimmie and ask him to explain it to him.... Jimmie was always there for Hank. They had a strained relationship in some ways but in other ways they were extremely close.

She explains that Jimmie lived just next door and he would come up to the office quite often. "Jimmie and Hank both had an incredible sense of humour. It was great listening to them exchange quips. They were alike in many ways, but I think Jimmie was more like Min. She had a soft demeanor, while Hank was a little more like a loose cannon! But there was no doubt about it, Jimmie loved his dad and Hank loved him!"

Reflecting on those years with Hank, Sheri describes the atmosphere at the office as usually upbeat and light.

> Hank got a kick out of the fact that we all talked about how tight he was with his money, but he still remembered what it was like to have nothing. He grew up that way and that was never very far from his mind...always cautioning us about being wasteful. I was opening some mail one day when he was standing at my desk and I threw a paperclip in the trash can. He looked surprised and I said, "Come on, Hank, it was bent!" He continued to give me that look and I said, "Do you want me to straighten it and put it back?" He did actually find that funny.

One day, she remembers, Hank came in the office carrying a penny gumball machine that Jimmie had given him as a gift. "He was so proud of it. It was on a stand and he set it up against the wall behind my desk and set a small container of pennies down on the table beside it. I said, 'I can't believe *you* are going to furnish the pennies.' He grinned and said, 'I'm not. This is just to make change.'"

When it came to helping other people, though, Hank had a heart of gold. "He helped so many people who came to him when they were down on their luck," says Sheri. "He said he knew what it was like to need a hand and he never asked for anything in return. He didn't want anyone to know about it. It was never talked about...just forgotten."

Sheri agrees that Hank did rub some people the wrong way, especially people who could not appreciate his sense of humour or understand his personality quirks.

> It just depends on who you talk to and what day they talked to Hank. Hank was like most other people—he could be arrogant, overbearing, and obnoxious all at the same time. Trust me, I know. I quit many times and was fired many more! He laughed about the number of times my keys sailed across the office at him. He was like most people I know, including me. He had good days and bad days. I always knew when he walked in what kind of mood he was in. I'm sure he would say the same thing about me. We were in the same room all day long and we knew how to push each other's buttons. That was not a big deal. But anyone who really knew Hank on a personal level would tell you that he was hilariously funny. You can't take that away from him. He was funny when he wasn't even trying. He just had that persona about him.

On the other hand, Sheri adds, there's no doubt that Hank had a fiery temper.

> The only person who could keep him in line, so to speak, was Min. All she had to do was not speak to him for a couple of days. She was a master at that. She would just go about life as if he wasn't in the house. Hank hated it! He would jump through hoops trying to get back in her good graces. Min was so cool! She would tell me, "Just ignore him." But that didn't work for me the way it did her...

it usually ended up getting me fired. That always meant a day or two off from work—I considered it a mini vacation—but I never missed a paycheque. One thing about Hank, though, he always accepted the blame because most of the time he didn't really remember how it started. Min told me later that Hank came in one day and asked, "Where's Sheri?" Min replied, "You fired her." Hank said, "Well that's no reason for her not to be at work!"

The one constant throughout Hank's life was his love for Minnie, and Sheri has many fond memories of her time at Rainbow Ranch with Hank's wife.

Min was such an important part of my everyday life. The office was located at the back of Hank's main residence, and it was just a walk from the office, through the studio, through a set of sliding doors into the main residence. Hank and Min made me feel so much at home over the years. I had access to every room in the house anytime I wanted to walk in. I could go in and sit down at the kitchen table, have coffee with Min or talk to her while she was baking. I could go into her bedroom if she was still in bed and we would sit watching TV or look at something she had found in a magazine. She was always there for me if I needed to talk. Or if I wanted her to come out into the office, I would just push the intercom and she would be there.

Rainbow Ranch was a great location to work, Sheri recalls.

Just as soon as the warm weather rolled around, Hank and I would move our office outside. We both loved the outdoors and we actually ran our office from poolside when it was nice. Hank did telephone interviews, had visitors, and did everything down by the pool just like we were in the office. I had the best working environment of anyone I knew. Hank enjoyed being outside so

Sheri and Hank at Rainbow Ranch.

much that he would often mow his own pasture. He had someone there who did that type of work but he just wanted to do it. You could see Hank over in the pasture and occasionally he would stop the mower and just sit there waiting for a snake to cross in front of the mower. He would never kill a snake. I've seen Hank stand on the office steps literally talking to the squirrels. He could make a sound just like them and they would answer. He loved animals. He always had dogs and cats. His trained horse, Shawnee, is buried on a beautiful spot in the pasture. That's one thing that was so nice about working there. Even though the house was in a residential neighbourhood, you just drove in a tree-lined driveway to the back of the residence and it was all in a very wooded, secluded area totalling about three acres. It was the most serene feeling. That's the reason Hank loved it so much.

In the early days Hank partied hard, and Sheri recalls he loved to tell stories about his exploits as a struggling performer. In later years he was more settled but still surrounded himself with people who could keep him laughing. He would often have what he called "tea parties" at the office with his buddies in the business, during which they'd laugh and carry on and generally just enjoy each other's company. In particular, Sheri says, Hank enjoyed kidding around with his good friend and fellow country music singer, Ferlin Husky.

> When Ferlin Husky would call, Hank would have me tell Ferlin that he didn't want to talk to him, that he would only talk to Simon [Simon Crum, Ferlin's comic alter ego]. Ferlin would put Simon on the phone. Simon always called Hank "Clarence." Sometimes when Hank would be sitting at his desk he would just reach over, pick up the phone and call Minnie Pearl. They would have a delightful conversation. He liked to hear her sing "Have I told you Lately That I Love You," and she would always sing that before she hung up the phone.

Although it has been many years since Sheri was last in the company of Hank Snow, he is still very dear to her. While her association with him may have started as his employee, in the end, she considered him to be a very close and personal friend.

> My memories of Hank are some of the best in my life. He was game for anything anybody wanted to do. I'll bet most of the people who ever spent any downtime with Hank will tell you the same thing. And that never changed. When I think of a way to describe Hank, I say he actually grew old without ever growing up! And that's not a bad thing. The last year or so for Hank was tough...for everyone, especially his family. And even though I wasn't with him every day during his final years, I talked to him enough to know that some of the Hank I knew was still there.

HANK'S LEGACY

I n a letter dated September 18, 1991, to Dr. Kenneth Ozmon, the president of Saint Mary's University in Halifax, Associate Professor Porter Scobey wrote, "Hank Snow's career has spanned more than half a century and produced an enormous body of work—both loved by his fans and respected by his peers—in the field of country music. In fact, it is generally agreed upon by those in country music that Canada has never produced anyone of that genre who combines the talents of singer, songwriter and musician quite as well as does Hank Snow."

In May 1994, the university bestowed upon Hank one of the highest honours he had ever received—an honorary Doctor of Letters

Hank Snow is congratulated by Dolly Parton following his induction into the Country Music Hall of Fame.

Hank receives his honorary degree from St. Mary's University in 1994 from Dr. Kenneth Ozmon, president of the university.

Canadian prime minister, Pierre Elliott Trudeau, inducts Hank Snow into the Juno Awards Canadian Music Hall of Fame in 1979.

(DLitt). The award was especially gratifying for Hank as it not only recognized his entire body of work, but also because it came from his home province.

Attempting to sum up the legacy of Hank Snow is no easy task. He was elected into seven halls of fame: Nashville Songwriters Hall of Fame (1978), Country Music Hall of Fame in Nashville (1979), Juno Awards Canadian Music Hall of Fame (1979), Canadian Hall of Honour (1985), Canadian Country Music Hall of Fame (1989), Nova Scotia Country Music Hall of Fame (1997, making him the first inductee along with Wilf Carter), and Canadian Songwriters Hall of Fame (2003). The list of his awards and accolades is long and impressive. His work has inspired countless other entertainers. Elvis Presley, The Rolling Stones, Ringo Starr, Ray Charles, Johnny Cash, and Emmylou Harris are among those who have either covered songs Hank had previously recorded or recorded those he wrote but never recorded himself.

(above) Hank Snow was in-
ducted into the Country Music
Hall of Fame and Museum in
Nashville in 1979.

(left) Hank Snow's Country
Music Hall of Fame plaque.

Influencing Today's Music

Years after his death, singers are still singing Hank Snow's songs. For instance, in the spring of 2013, two of Canada's top country music stars, Terri Clark and Dean Brody, released a new version of the Hank Snow classic, "I'm Movin' On." Of the song, Clark says:

> My dad's parents used to listen to Hank Snow all the time. Hank was the first Canadian Grand Ole Opry member, and I'm the only female Canadian Opry member so it feels like we have a bond. Dean just won Canadian Country Music Awards for Male Artist and Album of the Year. He opened a tour for me a few years ago in Canada. He drove his truck from town to town, in blizzards, from one end of the country to the other, to stand with his guitar for twenty minutes and get in front of people. I really admired his work ethic, that he was willing to go to those lengths to get his music in front of people, so I really wanted to have him on this song because it felt like a fitting tribute to Hank Snow.

Following Hank's death, singer-songwriter Mark Brine wrote a memorial to the country music legend that appeared on Hillbilly-Music.com: "Hank was that kind of man—real, super decent man! He was a top-rate person! A quiet man, which is often misread as a

Another sign of Hank's legacy in Liverpool.

stuck-up, etc. (for its reclusive similarities…) but he had a big heart. A good heart. One that had probably been abused by 'takers' in the past and so, the retreat. I am truly proud to have known him and blessed by his acquaintance."

So what is Hank Snow's legacy?

He was an international recording artist who sold millions of records; an award-winning songwriter who left behind a multitude of compositions; a generous philanthropist; a successful businessman; a loving and devoted husband and father; a dedicated son; a thoughtful employer; a loyal friend; a tireless advocate for abused and neglected children; a flashy showman; a champion for traditional country music; a world-class entertainer; a dreamer who dared to dream big and worked to realize those dreams.

Hometown Honours

In the end, Hank Snow's impressive body of work that influenced, and continues to influence, generations of musicians around the world will allow that legacy to live on in perpetuity. While organizations such as the Country Music Hall of Fame and Museum in Nashville will ensure that the legacy of Hank Snow is forever immortalized along with other legends of country music, efforts to remember the native son in his home province of Nova Scotia began in earnest in 1991, when a group calling themselves the Friends of Hank Snow Society organized a musical tribute in Hank's honour.

Eighth-annual Hank Snow Tribute held in Caledonia, Queens County.

Entertainers from throughout North America came to Liverpool to perform at the annual tribute. Note the guitar player second from the right is Roger Carol, one of two surviving members (as of 2014) of Hank Snow's Rainbow Ranch Boys.

This day of country music and celebrations subsequently grew into an annual festival known as the Hank Snow Tribute, which attracts fans of Hank Snow and of country music as well as entertainers from across North America and beyond. Although the tribute started as a small event on a white, sandy beach in Summerville, Queens County, after the first year it moved to the Queens County Fair Grounds in Caledonia to accommodate more spectators and to utilize the facilities there. In 1997, as the tribute became more successful and popular and began to draw larger audiences, it relocated to the South Shore Exhibition Grounds in nearby Bridgewater, Lunenburg County, where it was staged until 2013, when it was moved to Liverpool, near the museum that celebrates the life of Hank Snow.

Annual proceeds from the Hank Snow Tribute help finance the Hank Snow Home Town Museum, which officially opened in August 1997 and is operated by the Friends of Hank Snow Society. Located in the same historical train station where Hank spent many nights after sneaking away from his grandmother's house in Brooklyn to

Ribbon-cutting in August 1997 officially opening the Hank Snow Home Town Museum. Jimmie Rodgers Snow is third from the left.

go to Liverpool to visit his mother, the refurbished structure tells of Hank's amazing journey from his impoverished childhood to worldwide acclaim as one of the greats of country music. Exhibits at the museum highlight Hank's early Canadian career, his rise to international fame, and his incredible success at the Grand Ole Opry, as well as his personal life, including his marriage to Minnie Aalders and his efforts to abolish child abuse.

Along with the many treasured and personal artifacts on display at the museum are Hank's 1947 and 1974 Cadillac cars, two of his prized possessions, because, as Jimmie points out, no matter how much the family may have suffered financially, it was always important to his father that he look successful and driving an impressive vehicle was part of maintaining that image.

"His cars were important to him and it's fitting that they're on display at the museum," Jimmie says. Although Hank never had the occasion to see the museum first-hand, Jimmie says he knows his father was pleased and proud of what the society has established in his hometown. "My dad was very grateful for what they did for him. He felt very blessed for this honour." Likewise, Hank's long-time personal

The Hank Snow Home Town Museum in Liverpool, Nova Scotia.

assistant, Sheri Blackwood, says she's sure Hank was proud that his hometown recognized his achievements.

> I think that meant a lot to Hank because that train station meant a lot to him. He spent a lot of time there—a lot of nights—when he was a kid. Hanging over my desk in the office at Hank's place was a large picture of the station that was presented to Hank when they started working on the museum, and that reminded him of his past. He never forgot where he came from and what he went through, no matter how big he became.

Hank's beloved wife, Min, visits the Hank Snow Home Town Museum in Liverpool in August 2000.

Some people felt the efforts to recognize Hank Snow in his hometown were long overdue, and when I asked Hank in a July 1991 interview about that issue, he quickly answered, "I think it's wonderful. I don't think about whether or not it's long overdue, I just wish them all the very best luck and my heartfelt thanks for what they are doing. It's very exciting that some people would go to so much trouble to recognize me and I appreciate their efforts."

While Hank said it would have been an honour to attend the museum's opening, he admitted he wouldn't make it...and he never had the opportunity to see the facility in person. "I have quit the road and I don't travel much anymore," he said.

> It's been a few years since I've been back to Nova Scotia and right now I don't have any immediate plans to come back, but who can say what will happen in the future? I would not like to make a commitment to those kind people that I will be able to come back when it may not be possible. I guess we'll just have to wait and see when

the time comes, but again I wish them all the luck in their efforts and give them my support.

When asked how it felt knowing that people in his hometown, where it all started, were working to establish such local recognition for him, Hank quickly answered with a question of his own.

How should it feel? It feels wonderful and I'm grateful for those people who are doing it. I know there are some people who feel Canadians don't support the success of their own, but I don't really believe that's true. Of course you're going to find some who may not be supportive, but by and large the majority of people have given me a great deal of encouragement. The efforts of those people is just another way of them showing their support for me and I appreciate that. They have my blessing.

When Hank Snow died in December 1999, his death marked the end of an era, but his musical legacy continues to live on and these museums and monuments will preserve his memory so that future generations can learn the story of Hank Snow.

As Hank was fond of saying at the close of each of his performances, "Good luck, good health, and may the good Lord always be proud of you."

THE HANK SNOW STORY IN BRIEF

1914: Born in Brooklyn, Queens County, Nova Scotia, on May 9.

1922: Parents divorce.

1926: Goes to sea as a twelve-year-old cabin boy to escape abusive stepfather.

1929: Begins listening to his idol, Jimmie Rodgers.

1933: Moves to Halifax, gets his own radio show with CHNS, and begins to call himself "Hank, The Yodeling Ranger."

1935: Marries Minnie Blanche Aalders on September 2.

1936: Son Jimmie Rodgers Snow is born February 6, named after Hank's music idol; auditions for RCA on October 11, beginning the longest contract in history of recording industry.

1944: Starts playing in Hollywood featuring trick horse, Shawnee.

1945: Debuts on radio shows in Wheeling, West Virginia.

1948: Tours Texas as guest of country star Ernest Tubb, who starts crusade to bring Snow to the Grand Ole Opry.

1949: First U.S. release, "Brand On My Heart," scores first top single: "Marriage Vow."

1950: Debuts on the Grand Ole Opry on January 7; "I'm Movin' On" hits No. 1 later in the year (still holds the country music record for the number of consecutive weeks at No. 1: twenty-one).

1953: Loses his beloved mother, Marie Alice Boutlier; tours Korea with Tubb and plays to troops stationed there and in Japan.

1954: Begins working with Colonel Tom Parker. (Hank later ends this partnership on a bitter note with Tom when he learns that Parker signed rocker Elvis Presley to a personal management contract.)

1955: Records album with Chet Atkins.

1957: Is sworn in as U.S. citizen, January 27, at the Federal Courthouse in Nashville.

1962: "I've Been Everywhere" hits No. 1.

1974: Becomes the oldest country performer to have a No. 1 hit, "Hello Love," when he was sixty-one.

1975: Movie *Nashville* features a main character based in part on Hank Snow.

1978: Launches the Hank Snow Foundation for the Prevention of Child Abuse and Neglect of Children, Inc.; is inducted into the Songwriters Hall of Fame.

1979: Is inducted into the Country Music Hall of Fame in Nashville; also inducted into Canadian Academy of Recording Arts and Sciences Hall of Fame Canada by Prime Minister Trudeau at Juno Awards.

1980: Tours briefly with Kelly Foxton. Their duet "Hasn't It Been Good Together" marks his last billboard charting; meets with U.S. President Jimmy Carter to talk about his anti-child abuse efforts.

1981: Is dropped from RCA contract after forty-five years.

1984: Receives the Tree of Life Award from the Jewish National Fund for his work with abused children.

1985: Dissolves the Hank Snow Foundation and teams up with the National Exchange Club; records duet album with Willie Nelson, Hank's final label studio date; is inducted into Canadian Country Music Hall of Fame.

1986: Boycotts a CBS TV special on the Opry's sixtieth anniversary when producers limit his role to singing one verse of "I'm Movin' On"; celebrates his fiftieth year as a country music star; quits touring after doing a seven-day concert series in Nova Scotia.

1989: Makes final concert tour with show dates in Western Canada.

1991: Injures his knee in a car wreck driving to a Friday night Opry performance; the first Hank Snow Tribute is held on Summerville Beach in Queens County.

1994: Publishes autobiography, *The Hank Snow Story*, with University of Illinois Press; receives an honorary Doctorate of Letters Degree on his eightieth birthday from Saint Mary's University in Halifax.

1995: *The Hank Snow Story* chosen as a finalist in the country music category of the 1995 ARSC Awards of Excellence competition.

1996: Makes his final appearance on the Grand Ole Opry on Saturday, September 6.

1997: Becomes first inductee to the Nova Scotia Country Music Hall of Fame with Wilf Carter; Hank Snow Tribute relocates to the South Shore Exhibition Grounds in nearby Bridgewater, Lunenburg County.

1999: Hank Snow dies on December 20 at his home in Madison, Tennessee, at age eighty-five.

2003: Hank's widow, Minnie Snow, dies of pneumonia at age eighty-nine on May 12; Hank's inaugural induction into the Canadian Songwriters Hall of Fame on December 3.

2013: Annual Hank Snow Tribute moves back to Liverpool after previously being held in Summerville, Caledonia, and Bridgewater.

HANK SNOW RECORDING HISTORY

Number One Singles

Year	Song	Weeks #1	Weeks Chart
1950	I'm Movin' On	21	44
1950	The Golden Rocket	2	23
1951	Rhumba Boogie	8	27
1954	I Don't Hurt Anymore	20	41
1954	Let Me Go, Lover	2	16
1962	I've Been Everywhere	2	22
1974	Hello Love	1	15

Recording Achievements

Total Singles Charted: 85

Top 40 Chart Hits: 65

Top 10 Chart Hits: 43

No. 1 Chart Hits: 7

Total Weeks on Charts: 876

Total Weeks at no. 1: 56

Total Albums Released: 120

Hank Snow Albums

1950: *I'm Movin' On/With This Ring I Thee Wed, The Golden Rocket/Paving The Highway With Tears, Somewhere Along Life's Highway/Within This Broken Heart Of Mine*

1951: *Favorites*

1952: *My Mother/I Just Telephone Upstairs, Hank Snow Sings, Married By The Bible, Divorced By The Law/Lady's Man*

1953: *I Don't Hurt Anymore*

1954: *Cryin', Prayin', Waitin', Hopin'/I'm Glad I Got To See You Once Again, Country Pickin'*

1955: *Hank Snow's Country Guitar, Country Classics, Would You Mind?/Yellow Roses*

1956: *Hula Rock/Conscience I'm Guilty*

1957: *Country & Western Jamboree*

1959: *The Singing Ranger, When Tragedy Struck*

1961: *Hank Snow's Souvenirs, The Southern Cannonball, Big Country Hits: Songs I Hadn't Recorded Till Now*

1962: *Ancient History/I've Been Everywhere, Together Again The One And Only Hank Snow*

1963: *I've Been Everywhere, The Man Who Robbed The Bank At Santa Fe, Railroad Man, More Hank Snow Souvenirs*

1964: *The Old And Great Songs, Songs Of Tragedy*

1965: *"The Highest Bidder" And Other Favorites*

1966: *The Best Of*

1967: *Snow In Hawaii*

1968: *Born For You/The Late And Great Love (Of My Heart), My Nova Scotia Home*

1971: *(The Seashores Of) Old Mexico*

1973: *Snowbird*

1974: *Hello Love, Famous Country Music Makers: Vol. II*

1975: *All About Trains*

1992: *Snow Country*

2000: *Blues For My Blue Eyes*

2004: *The Singing Ranger, All American Country*

2006: *Greatest Hits & Favorites*

2011: *Songs Of Tragedy/When Tragedy Struck*

Hank Snow Songbook

1950
I'm Movin' On
Paving The Highway With Tears
Somewhere Along Life's
　　Highway
The Golden Rocket
Within This Broken Heart of
　　Mine
With This Ring I Thee Wed
You Broke The Chain That Held
　　Our Hearts

1951
My Two Timin' Woman
No Golden Tomorrow Ahead
Wasted Love

1952
Confused With The Blues
Golden River
I Just Telephone Upstairs
I Knew That We'd Meet Again
(I Wished Upon) My Little
　　Golden Horseshoe
Lady's Man
Married By The Bible, Divorced
　　By The Law
Moanin'
My Mother
(Now And Then There's) A Fool
　　Such As I
On That Old Hawaiian Shore
　　With You

The Gal Who Invented Kissin'
Yodeling Cowboy
Zeb Turney's Gal

1953
I Don't Hurt Anymore
My Arabian Baby

1954
Hilo March
Cryin', Prayin', Waitin', Hopin'
Wabash Blues
Sweet Marie
I'm Glad I Got To See You Once
　　Again
In An Old Dutch Garden

1955
Bluebird Island
Down The Trail Of Achin'
　　Hearts
Madison Madness
Marriage Vow
Music Makin' Mama From
　　Memphis
Rainbow Boogie
The Rhumba Boogie
Twelfth Street Rag
Unwanted Sign Upon Your Heart
Vaya Con Dios (May God Be
　　With You)
Would You Mind?
Yellow Roses

1956

Conscience I'm Guilty

Hula Rock

1957

Among My Souvenirs

Born To Lose

I Almost Left My Mind

It's Been So Long Darling

Loose Talk

Memories Are Made Of This

My Life With You

Poison Love

Sing Me A Song Of The Islands

Singing The Blues

These Tears

Wedding Bells

1959

Ben Dewberry's Final Run

Born To Be Happy

Don't Make Me Go To Bed And
    I'll Be Good

Honeymoon On A Rocket Ship

The Gold Rush Is Over

I Cried But My Tears Were Too
    Late

I'm Gonna Bid My Blues
    Goodbye

I'm Here To Get My Baby Out
    Of Jail

I Went To Your Wedding

Just A Faded Petal From A
    Beautiful Boquet

Little Buddy

Mississippi River Blues

Nobody's Child

Old Shep

Put My Little Shoes Away

The Convict & The Rose

The Drunkard's Child

The Engineer's Child

The Letter Edged In Black

The Night I Stole Old Sammy
    Morgan's Gin

The Prisoner's Prayer

There's A Little Box Of Pine On
    The 7.29

1961

Address Unknown

A Legend In My Time

A Petal From A Faded Rose

Bury Me Deep

Fräulein

I Care No More

I'll Go On Alone

I'm Movin' In

I Love You Because

Let Me Go, Lover!

Mansion On The Hill

My Blue Eyed Jane

Panamama

Return To Me

Send Me The Pillow You Dream
    On

Tangled Mind

That Heart Belongs To Me

The Boogie Woogie Flying Cloud

There Wasn't An Organ At Our
    Wedding

These Hands
The Southern Cannonball
Trouble, Trouble, Trouble
Under The Double Eagle
When Mexican Joe Met Jole Blon

1962

Ancient History
Anniversary Blue Yodel (Blue
    Yodel No. 7)
A Pair Of Broken Hearts
Carnival of Venice
For Sale
Hobo Bill's Last Ride
I Dreamed Of An Old Love
    Affair
If It's Wrong To Love You
I Never Will Marry
I've Been Everywhere
I Wonder Where You Are
    Tonight
Lazy Bones
Let's Pretend
Mockin' Bird Hill
My Adobe Hacienda
No Letter Today
Old Doc Brown (Just A Closer
    Walk With Thee)
Promised To John
Rose Of Old Monterey
Spanish Fire Ball
The Drunkard's Son
The Wreck Of The Old '97
Unfaithful
When My Blue Moon Turns To
    Gold Again

1963

Big Wheels
Chattanooga Choo Choo
Galway Bay
Geisha Girl
Ghost Train
Jamaica Farewell
In The Blue Canadian Rockies
It's A Little More Like Heaven
Lili Marlene
Lonesome Whistle
Melba From Melbourne
Miller's Cave
My Filipino Rose
One More Ride
Pan American
Southbound
Stolen Moments
The Change Of The Tides
The Crazy Engineer
The Last Ride
The Man Who Robbed The Bank
    At Santa Fe
The Next Voice You Hear
The Streamline
The Wreck Of Number Nine
Waiting For A Train
Way Out There
When It's Springtime in Alaska
You're Losing Your Baby
You're The Reason

1964

Brand On My Heart
Down Where The Dark Waters
    Flow

In Memory Of You Dear Old Pal
Little Joe
Mother I Thank You For The
	Bible You Gave
My Blue River Rose
My Sweet Texas Blue Bonnet
	Queen
Old Rover
Put Your Arms Around Me
Rocking Alone In An Old
	Rocking Chair
The Answer To Little Blossom
The Blue Velvet Band
The Color Song
The Prisoner's Dream
The Prisoner's Song
There's A Star Spangled Banner
	Waving Somewhere
The Texas Cowboy
Walking The Last Mile
Wanderin' On
We'll Never Say Goodbye, Just
	So Long
Within This Broken Heart of
	Mine
Your Little Band Of Gold

1965
My Arms Are A House
The Highest Bidder
The Only Rose

1966
Ninety Miles An Hour

1967
Beyond The Reef
Blue For Old Hawaii
Don't Sing Aloha When I Go
Hawaiian Cowboy
Hawaiian Sunset (Instrumental)
Hula Love

My Little Grass Shack In
	Kealakekua, Hawaii
Oahu Rose
On The Beach At Waikiki
The Crying Street Guitar Waltz
To You Sweetheart, Aloha
Trade Winds

1968
Born For You
Don't Hang Around Me Anymore
Just Across The Bridge Of Gold
Love Entered The Iron Door
My Nova Scotia Home
She's A Rose From The Garden
	Of Prayer
Squid Jiggin' Grounds
The Broken Wedding Ring
The Late And Great Love (Of
	My Heart)
The Soldier's Last Letter
The End Of The World
Too Many Tears

1971
No One Will Ever Know
(The Seashores of) Old Mexico

1973

Cool Water
Heart Break Trail
Peach Picking Time Down In
    Georgia
Snowbird
Tumbling Tumbleweeds

1974

A Daisy A Day
Hello Love
Honeymoon On A Rocketship
How To Play The Guitar
I Have You And That's Enough
    For Me (Part 1)
I Have You And That's Enough
    For Me (Conclusion)
In An 18th Century Drawing
    Room
It Just Happened That Way
It's Only You, Only You, That I
    Love
I've Forgotten You
I've Got To Give It All To You
I Washed My Hands In Muddy
    Waters (Part 1)
I Washed My Hands In Muddy
    Waters (Conclusion)
I Will Never Marry
Jimmie The Kid
No Longer A Prisoner
Silver Bells
Somewhere My Love
Star Spangled Waltz
The First Nighters
The Last Thing On My Mind

The Mystery Of Number Five
The Old Spinning Wheel
Today I Started Loving You
    Again
When Jimmie Rodgers Said
    Goodbye
Why Did You Give Me Your Love
Why Me, Lord

1975

Fire Ball Mail
The Brakeman's Blues
The City Of New Orleans
Train Whistle Blues
Wabash Cannonball

1992

A Woman Captured Me
Breakfast With The Blues
Doggone That Train
I Stepped Over The Line
I've Cried A Mile
Ninety Miles An Hour (Down A
    Dead End Street)
The Restless One
Whispering Rain
You Take The Future (And I'll
    Take The Past)

2000

Barefoot Blues (Blue Yodel No.
    12)
Blue Christmas
Blue Dreams
Blue Eyes Crying In The Rain

Blue Rose Of The Rio
Bye Bye Blues
Frankie And Johnny
I Almost Lost My Mind
I'm Thinking Tonight Of My Blue
    Eyes
My Good Gal's Gone
Never No Mo' Blues
Ninety-Nine Year Blues
These Tears Are Not For You
Those Blue Eyes Don't Sparkle
    Anymore
Travellin' Blues
Trouble In Mind
Tuck Away My Lonesome Blues
You Nearly Lose Your Mind

2004
I'm Sending You Red Roses
Lonesome Blue Yodel
Love's Game Of Let's Pretend
Wandering On

My San Antonio Mama
The Anniversary Of My Broken
    Heart
The Hobo's Last Ride
Your Locket Is My Broken Heart

2006
Can't Have You Blues
Caribbean
For Now And Always
He'll Understand And Say Well
    Done
Mainliner (The Hawk Of The
    West)
The Crazy Mambo Thing
There's A Picture On Pinto's
    Bridle
Unwanted Sign Upon My Heart

2011
The Runt

BIBLIOGRAPHY

Currie, Brian. "Return of The Singing Ranger." *The 4ᵗʰ Estate*, May 19, 1976.

Eipper, Laura. "Snow's meet with Carter: 'Real fine.'" *The Tennessean*, January 29, 1980.

"Hank Snow's widow dies of pneumonia." *The Tennessean*, May 2003.

"Hank Snow Still 'Movin' On.'" *The Advance*, September 23, 1970.

"Hank the Singing Ranger Coming." *The Advance*, August 1, 1946.

"Hank Snow in good health; rebuts son's comments." *The Chronicle Herald*, August 29, 1996.

Littleton, Bill. "MCN visits Snow's Rainbow Ranch." *Music City News,* April 1976.

Loggins, Kirk. "Dementia clouded Snow's last year." *The Tennessean*, January 20, 2000.

McMaHahan, Ken. "The Singing Ranger Hank Snow." *Country Music Greats*, Winter 2000.

"Mrs. Charles Tanner [Obituary]." *The Advance*, October 21, 1953.

Oickle, Vernon. "Hank Snow returns after 45 year absence." *The Advance*, July 21, 1982.

———. "Native son: Country music legend Hank Snow excited by local committee's efforts." *The Advance*, July 17, 1991.

Porteous, John. "Hank Snow, country singer." *Atlantic Insight*, May 1980.

Quill, Greg. "Hank Snow moves on." *The Toronto Star*, December 21, 1999.

Slotek, Jim. "Snow Movin' On: Country legend dies at 85." *The Toronto Sun*, December 21, 1999.

Smith, Tom. "Country singer Hank Snow: I am raising money to help battered children—because I was one." *The National Enquirer*, n.d.

"Snow accepts SMU degree on tape." *The Daily News*, May 10, 1994.

"Snow dead at 85." *The Chronicle Herald*, December 21, 1999.

Snow, Hank. "A message from Hank Snow." *Hank Snow Folio*, 1951.

———. "In Memory of Jimmie." *Country Song Roundup*, July 1955.

Snow, Hank, Jack Ownbey, and Bob Burris. *The Hank Snow Story.* Urbana: University of Illinois Press, 1994.

"Snow mourned at the Opry." *The Toronto Star*, December 26, 1999.

"Three honored for community work." *Saint Mary's Times*, May 1994.

Orr, Jay, Robert K. Oermann. "Country music legend Hank Snow moves on: 'Opry' pillar is dead at 85." *The Tennessean*, December 21, 1999.

Orr, Jay. "'Singing Ranger' recalled: Hank Snow mourners pay tribute." *The Tennessean*. December 24, 1999.

Websites

wsws.org

countryuniverse.net

vernondalhart.com

hillbilly-music.com

countrymusictreasures.com

countrypolitan.com

countrymusichalloffame.org